John Bossy

Christianity in the West
1400 – 1700

D0060741

Oxford   New York

OXFORD UNIVERSITY PRESS

1985

Oxford University Press, Walton Street, Oxford OX2 6DP

London New York Toronto
Delhi Bombay Calcutta Madras Karachi
Kuala Lumpur Singapore Hong Kong Tokyo
Nairobi Dar es Salaam Cape Town
Melbourne Auckland
and associated companies in
Beirut Berlin Ibadan Mexico City Nicosia

Oxford is a trade mark of Oxford University Press

British Library Cataloguing in Publication Data

Bossy, John
Christianity in the West 1400–1700.—(OPUS)
1. Church history—Middle Ages, 600–1500
2. Church history—Modern period, 1500–
I. Title   II. Series
209 BR270

ISBN 0-19-219174-8
ISBN 0-19-289162-6 Pbk

Library of Congress Cataloging in Publication Data

Bossy, John.
Christianity in the West, 1400–1700. (OPUS)
Bibliography: p.   Includes index.
1. Christianity—Middle Ages, 600–1500.   2. Christianity—16th century.
I. Title.   II. Series.
BR280.B6   1985   274'.05   84-20714

ISBN 0-19-219174-8
ISBN 0-19-289162-6 (pbk.)

Set by Wyvern Typesetting Ltd., Bristol
Printed in Great Britain by
Richard Clay (The Chaucer Press) Ltd.
Bungay, Suffolk

An OPUS book

Christianity in the West
1400–1700

OPUS General Editors

Keith Thomas
Alan Ryan
Peter Medawar

For Mary and for Nick,
after twenty years

'The Tigers of Wrath are wiser than the Horses of Instruction.'
William Blake, *The Marriage of Heaven and Hell*

Preface

For most of the time I have been writing this book, I have thought of it as carrying the subtitle, 'an essay'. Persuaded for several excellent reasons that this would not do, I record here my feeling that the book possesses something of the partiality and over-systematic character of that genre. I should also like to explain one or two things about it which may be disconcerting. Its subject is Christianity, by which I mean that it is not about the Church restrictively defined: it is about a body of people, a way or ways of life and the features of Christian belief which seemed most relevant to them. Its boundaries are those which separate Greek or Orthodox Christianity from the Latin West, though I fear that Slav, Magyar, Scandinavian and Irish Christianity are poorly represented. Its limits in time are a pair of dates roughly indicating the topic aimed at. One way of describing this would be to say that it was the Reformation considered as an event in human life, and that the dates were intended to sketch the minimum space, before and after, within which some kind of purchase on the event might be obtained. This cannot quite be an adequate description, since I have devoted slightly over half the book to what I have called, I hope with a proper sense of the pitfalls involved, 'traditional Christianity'. I do not think the emphasis actually incompatible with the description, but it is probably simpler to defend on other grounds. These are: first, that it covers most of the field, since nearly everybody in the West before the Reformation, and prob-ably most people after it, were traditional Christians; second, that a fairly systematic description of this tradition has been a long-felt want in the history of late medieval and early modern Europe; and, third, that the intellectual climate seems now a good deal sunnier towards it than it used to be, and the prospect of saying interesting things about it is brighter.

This bias towards the traditional has entailed a degree of sympathetic or beneficial interpretation which, despite my good

intentions, I have not always managed to extend to the efforts of
those who sought to improve it. But this is not the main reason why
my account of the sixteenth century is somewhat partial. I ask the
reader to imagine it as an attempt to answer the question: 'Supposing that your account of what you call traditional Christianity is
roughly correct, what difference does it make to the conventional
narrative of sixteenth-century reformations, Protestant or
Catholic?' If he finds that in trying to expound that difference I
have ironed out some of the nuances between versions of reformed
Christianity, I hope he will take the rest of the book as witness that
I do actually believe theological or ecclesiastical distinctions to be
important and historically creative. My defence here is that attention to family resemblances between the forms of Christianity born
or reconstructed in the sixteenth century seemed to allow for a
more enlightening answer to the question posed. I think it more
likely that I have overdone the resemblance, than that by passing
over regional individualities I have exaggerated the unity of pre-
Reformation Christianity.

Given these preoccupations, I have tried to be descriptive, to
save the phenomena I knew about; where explanation is implied, as
in parts of Chapter 6, it should be taken, to borrow a phrase from
Clifford Geertz, more as a contribution to the thickness of the
description than as the key to open a door upon the mysteries of
change. I should like to have stuck up for the reality of the past as
something actually there, not as the proverbial nose of wax begging
to be remodelled according to the artistic canons or surgical
technology of the present. Among disfigurements of this piece of
the past I count the idea that medieval Christianity was a burden
which most of the population of the West was delighted to shake
off; or that there was something you can call 'popular culture' and
distinguish radically from something called 'élite culture', especially where that popular culture is held by axiom to be non-
Christian; or that Christianity was brought to the people of the
West during and after the sixteenth century. One effect of proceed-
ing in a descriptive frame of mind is to diminish the appeal of such
gratuitous assumptions. My own gratuitous assumptions will be
plain enough. One of them is intimated in the quotation from Blake
which I have ventured to place over the threshold of the book. I say
'ventured', because to call upon Blake is to handle an explosive
substance which may easily blow up in your face. If I have

mistreated him he will be avenged, but it seemed worth the risk.

From the secret multitude of the book's benefactors I should like to remember Margaret Aston, Dermot Fenlon and Diane Hughes; Keith Thomas, who proposed it; and Hilary Feldman, who has edited it. It also owes a lot to two remarkable collections of people: the members of the Institute for Advanced Study at Princeton, and of the nearby Davis Center, in whose company it was begun in September 1976; and the history students of the University of York, without whom it would have been finished a good deal sooner than it has been. I have been a sort of bottleneck between them.

JOHN BOSSY

York
June 1984

Contents

PART ONE

Traditional Christianity

1   Christ, Mary and the Saints

The year 1400 is an appropriate point to begin a description of the Christianity which confronted the reformers of the sixteenth century, for it was a year in which nothing much happened. For twenty years the Church had been suffering from the Great Schism of the West, and would continue in that state for another seventeen. There were two popes, one of whom spent the year shut up in his palace at Avignon, the other in the Castel Sant'Angelo in Rome. Schism was the prevalent disorder of the time, and also the most unnerving. It meant division, hatred and conflict in what should have been the centre of unity and peace. People were alarmed that it had happened, and the more sensitive were upset by the fear that everyone would get used to it. It imperilled their earthly welfare and their prospects of eternal salvation. It provoked the wrath of God, and since they had been bearing for fifty years the stigma of bubonic plague they had reason to fear what else God's anger might have in store for them. One thing which did not happen in 1400 was the expected Jubilee, or general amnesty for sin, granted to those who made the pilgrimage to Rome. Pope Boniface VIII had inaugurated this universal boon in 1300, and had intended it to happen once a century; but the preoccupations of the last Roman pope had caused him to anticipate it in 1390. None the less, thousands of people turned up in Rome for a Jubilee which had not been proclaimed. Which goes to show that the Christians of the late medieval West did not need reformers to tell them who their saviour was: not the pope, nor the learned Fathers of the Council of Constance who finally settled the Schism in 1417; not even, in the end, the hierarchical Church itself, but Christ.

The theory of salvation they were working on had been expounded by St Anselm of Canterbury three hundred years before. In the Garden of Eden, it went, Adam and Eve had disobeyed God. In so doing they had erected between themselves and him a state of offence which had entailed their exclusion from paradise; this state had been transmitted to their descendants. God, according to justice, could not cease to be offended, or restore man to his favour, until a compensation had been paid and his honour repaired. Man therefore owed a debt of restitution to God, but had not the wherewithal to pay it, since the whole world would not have sufficed to compensate for the offence, and man had nothing to offer which was not God's anyway.

Only God himself could satisfy the debt; but since the satisfaction was owed by man, a lawful offer of it could only be made by someone who was both God and man. The gospels testified, in face of the scepticism of those of other faiths, that the existence of so necessary a person was a fact of history. The Church, after much thought, had determined that his existence entailed the eternal presence of a plurality of persons in God, and so its creeds affirmed. Out of the Father, the Son and the Holy Ghost, for us men and for our salvation, the Son had taken upon himself to be born among the generation of Adam and Eve, and to offer spontaneously to the Father the death to which he was not subject in due satisfaction for the offence of his kin. And just as the offence of Adam and Eve was so great that the whole world was inadequate to compensate for it, so the weight of compensation which Christ might claim for his death was more than the world might ever contain. Not needing it himself, he asked the Father that the debt be transferred to his fellow men, which the Father could not in justice refuse. So man was able at length to make satisfaction, to abolish the state of offence between himself and God, and to be restored to favour and future beatitude.

If we could consider this story as one we had never heard before, we might be struck by two axioms. There is the axiom about satisfaction: that offences which occur in a relationship between two parties can only be regulated, and the previous state of relations between them restored, by an act of retributive compensation equal in weight to the offence committed. It could be argued that there is also a theory about merit, where the rule of satisfaction applies in a more abstract way, and by anticipation, to offences which may not yet have been committed; so that, in a relation between two or more parties, a second party who undergoes painful or disagreeable experiences acquires, in respect of the first, a credit in a moral currency which he may then spend himself or transfer to a third. There must be something in the idea expounded by Nietzsche in *The Genealogy of Morals* that ascetic behaviour, like the Irish custom of fasting against one's enemies, is always in some fundamental way aggressive, and that theories of meritorious suffering refer back, via assumptions about satisfaction, to the instinct of legitimate vengeance. The meek Lamb of the Apocalypse is also a vehicle of wrath. But though Anselm had precedents in the Church Fathers for treating the Redemption as illustrating a theory of merit, his own reading of it remains that of a particular satisfaction proportionate to a particular state of offence, and it took later theologians like Aquinas to elaborate a general theory of the circulation of merit.

The only axiom Anselm requires, besides the rule of satisfaction, is an axiom about kinship: that in the commission and resolution of offences those who are related to the offender by generation are involved. They inherit the breach of relations with the party offended, and the debt of satisfaction which is owed to him; by the same token they may substitute themselves for the offending party in offering satisfaction, and if the satisfaction offered is adequate to the offence, there is an obligation on the party offended to accept it. As applied to the Redemption, the first part of the axiom, about the commission of offences, simply states the doctrine of original sin universally accepted among Christians. The second part, about their resolution, would seem to be an invention of Anselm's own, and it seems unlikely that St Paul, to whom he was in a sense appealing, would have approved of it. Among the Latin Fathers, Augustine had expounded the Christian implications of kinship in relation to marriage, and Ambrose in relation to charity. Neither of them had, so far as I know, discussed the effects of kinship in the satisfaction of offences, and this appears to have been Anselm's particular contribution. His account of the Redemption was by no means a necessary one and, like his proof of the existence of God, did not always prove acceptable, even to medieval theologians. It might appear to be incompatible with a belief in God's love, or to make the Resurrection superfluous. In putting it forward Anselm claimed not even to be speaking as a Christian theologian, but advancing an interpretation which he thought would be found instinctively persuasive by all men. But it remained in essentials the reading of the myth as it was understood by the average Christian in the later Middle Ages. Since it was found convincing, one may take it that the axioms it concealed were axioms which operated in the West from Anselm's day to Luther's.

I do not think we need enquire where they had come from or what, in the plumbing of the Western mind, their underground connection with each other may have been. We shall be concerned with the description of consequences, of which the most momentous for Western history has been pointed out by critical theologians. In Anselm's reading, the redeemer is Christ the man, not Christ as God. That with which he satisfies the Father is his godhead, but he who is satisfying must be man. Godhead is a sort of quantity with which Christ operates, a mysterious possession of the man. This was certainly how his double nature appeared to the average Christian of the late Middle Ages, for whom Christ was simply 'God'. In seeking to assure himself of his redemption, his principal concern was to know that this God was an actual man, from whose redeeming sacrifice he was accordingly entitled to benefit. The larger part of the imaginative resources of late medieval Christendom was devoted to embedding this idea in recognisable reality.

Christ had in the first place suffered. One knew why. One knew when and where, as could be verified by a visit to Jerusalem. One also knew how: by violent physical pain inflicted by other men on a man who in taking up his burden 'had not imagined such ferocity in the sons of Adam'. He had suffered by the flagellation, the crowning with thorns, the carrying of the cross, the crucifixion on Calvary recounted in the gospel narratives of the Passion, and by other pains recorded in the devout imagination of visionaries or the *Meditations on the Life of Christ* supposed to have been written by the Franciscan St Bonaventure. In such sources, avid for detail but concerned for authenticity, one might find the wiping of Christ's face by Veronica, the pain as his robe was torn off to reopen the wounds of the scourging, the deposition, the lamentation of Mary. The victorious standard of Constantine, the symbolic cross of the Greeks, was here a fifteen-foot piece of genuine timber, intolerably painful to carry, a socket for nails, bearer of a human body dying in a misery of blood, sweat and tears, of a human soul stunned by injustice and desolation. The cross remained the exterior symbol of Christianity, but the image of the Redemption became the crucifix, arms hanging, the crown of thorns still clamped to the head of the crucified. There could be no limit to the *pietà* or compassion which such fraternal piety must inspire. During the fifteenth century compassion would be stimulated for those of dimmer light by a holy refuse of splinters, thorns, shrouds and phials of blood, and for the more sophisticated by a cultivation of the interior imagination; it would inspire the efforts of painter and sculptor, later of woodcutter and engraver, and of the performers in mystery plays. In 1400 Christ's sufferings were the theme of a pullulation of passionate or macabre fictions, which it took a century or so to reduce to the relative order of the Stations of the Cross and the Sorrowful Mysteries of the Rosary.

By comparison the Nativity would be cultivated in something of a minor key. Certainly Christ had been a real baby, and would henceforth be represented in a more or less realistic nudity. St Bridget of Sweden had been told the physical details of the birth by the Virgin herself, and her account had transformed the way in which the scene was envisaged: Mary, kneeling, adores the infant projected from her womb on to the straw of the stable floor, before placing him in the manger where the breath of the ox and the ass will warm him. There was plenty in the situation to inspire emotion: Mary breast-feeding, lulling the child to sleep, teaching him to walk or read. In the words of a contemporary hymn

> *Parvum quando cerno Deum*
> *Matris inter brachia*
> *Colliquescit pectus meum*
> *Inter mille gaudia.*
>
> (When I see my little God
> In his mother's arms
> My heart is melted
> By a thousand joys.)[1]

The focus of such emotions, and certainly of older ones, Christmas was a great feast; the invention of the crib, apparently by St Francis in the thirteenth century, and of the carol in fifteenth-century England, testify that it was rising in the calendar. But it was still more a season than a day, and the signs are that, as a feast of Christ, it was at the close of the Middle Ages a good deal less popular than Good Friday.

Considering the obsession with Christ's humanity, this calls for some explanation. There was in the first place the difficulty of envisaging the physical facts of a virgin birth, which St Bridget had rather increased: it would have improved the action of the mystery plays if the apocryphal midwives, sensibly fetched by Joseph, could have been found something to do. One must also, I think, appeal to the idea that in 1400 it was still rather difficult for people to envisage childhood as a distinct stage of life: a mythology of the Christ-child was emerging, but its great days, like those of the crib and the carol, were in the future. The heart melted not quite so much for the child as child, as for the future victim of the Passion: the tenderness of the Coventry Carol, for those who first heard it, was less in the lullaby than in the threat from the raging King Herod which interrupted it, and the feast of the Innocents was certainly as well-marked a day in the Christmas season as the Nativity itself. To show, in the fifteenth century, that Christ was a real man, it was not necessary to resort to biology, and not sufficient to see that he was a child of known parents: it was necessary to know that he was someone with a human kin.

Of those kin Mary was the nearest, she who had the most right to rail against the rest of mankind for the killing of her son. As such, and despite some contrary indications in the gospels, she was bound to represent the first member of the redeemed human race. Out of the variety of ways in which Christians have tried to penetrate the implications of this fact there were two which now particularly throve. They were in one sense complementary, in another contradictory. The doctrine of Mary's immaculate conception affirmed that from the beginning of her existence she had been liberated from the common curse inherited by the children of Adam. It had been envisaged by Anselm and Aquinas, but rejected by them as incompatible with the doctrine of the Redemption. It had been taken up with great enthusiasm by the Franciscans: Dominicans therefore opposed it, and seem to have encouraged the portrayal of the Virgin suckling the child as a counterblast: it could be argued that, despite or perhaps because of its association with human kindness, the giving of milk was, like menstruation, an effect of Adam's curse. Since, as Calvin remarked with distaste, there seemed to be an awful lot of the Virgin's milk about on the eve of the Reformation, the Dominicans must have struck a chord; nevertheless the tide was against them, and the Immaculate Conception acquired an official feast-day and the honour of the Sistine

Chapel from the Franciscan Pope Sixtus IV, while the Virgin's milk eventually found refuge in the wine trade.

We need to remember that what was proposed for veneration was Mary's conception, not her birth, even though, according to the best opinion of the schools, the soul did not enter the embryo until forty days later. In the context of its time the doctrine referred to an event in sacred history which needed no further mention for contemporaries, and for moderns is classically illustrated in the version painted by Giotto shortly after 1300 on the walls of the Scrovegni Chapel in Padua. Here Anne and Joachim meet with a loving embrace outside the Golden Gate at Jerusalem and so providentially, perhaps miraculously, but certainly through the normal physical channels conceive the child Mary. There is nothing about the event in Matthew, Mark, Luke or John; but it forms the crux of the apocryphal gospels whose narratives were current through the version preserved in the much-read *Golden Legend* of Jacobus de Voragine, a history of salvation in the West in the form of a dictionary of saints. The value of this source was that it enabled Mary, and therefore Jesus, to appear in the world embedded in that plausible nexus of blood-relations on which, though satisfying about her cousinage to Elizabeth and John the Baptist, the canonical gospels gave such scanty and contradictory information.

According to the *Golden Legend* Elizabeth was Mary's cousin on her father's, Joachim's, side; but St Anne, despite her advanced years at the birth of Mary, had married twice again after Joachim's death. By her second husband she had had Mary Cleophas, the mother of the apostles James, Simon and Jude, described in the canonical gospels as Jesus' brethren. By her third she had had Mary Salome, who had married Zebedee: they were the parents of the other apostle James, and of John the Evangelist. From the point of view of the average fifteenth-century soul, and indeed of the model of contemporary Christian learning, the chancellor of the University of Paris, Jean Gerson, this was more like it: it made the dry narrative of the gospels a good deal more like life as they understood it. Anyone could now see that the wedding feast at Cana had been given by Zebedee and the third Mary, the Virgin's step-sister, for their son John the Evangelist. Mary the Virgin, as senior sister, was evidently in charge; it was natural that Jesus, for all his prudish reservations, would help with the supply of drink, though not surprising that he should carry the Evangelist off to virginity once the feast was over. Similarly, it was perfectly natural that Jesus should particularly love his step-cousin John, and should commend him to Mary on the cross, to take him as her son in lieu of himself; just as it had been for the older cousin John the Baptist to go out and prepare people for Jesus' coming. So the trinity of baptism, marriage and death were encompassed in the life of the Saviour by a proper complement of kin, and Mary's lament at the deposition could properly conclude it, as would that of any mother at her child's wake. At the head of this ramifying kindred stood the matriarchal figure of St Anne: the intensity with which her sanctity was cultivated in the fifteenth century testified to a general satisfaction that Christ had not come a foundling into the world. By 1500 there was a well-established mass for the veneration of St Anne and all her relations, and the entire *Heilige Sippe* or Holy Kindred was, as in Victorian photographs, an accepted object of the painter's art in the north. In the south, more conscious of form, it was represented by the trio of St Anne, Mary and the child Jesus dear to Leonardo.

It was certainly a matrilineal kindred: the line of generativity did not run strongly in the Holy Family. Joachim had been rejected from the temple for failure to beget; Joseph, in the tradition which the mystery plays expounded, was a doddering ancient, an unwilling spouse and a jealous husband, whose conviction that his wife had committed adultery inspired scenes a good deal more lively than those of the Nativity itself. The close of the Middle Ages was to see a remarkable rehabilitation of this dismal figure. Gerson launched the idea of Joseph as a saint. Soon afterwards he acquired a feast-day; by 1500 his cult was spreading from the carpenters' gilds to the population at large, and he had achieved the more youthful persona suitable to paternity. By the time of the Reformation, among those concerned to contain their devotion within authentic scriptural data, the new trinity of Jesus, Mary and Joseph was coming to rival the older one of Jesus, Mary and St Anne. The cultivation of the name Jesus, much promoted from the middle of the fifteenth century, was a tribute to it, since it was the name which Joseph had been instructed to give his wife's child; so, more sensationally, was the discovery about 1470 that the family house at Nazareth had been transported by air to the Italian village of Loreto a century or two before. Here was indeed a novel conception of the Holy Family: invented from scratch in the fifteenth century, and promoted by the post-Reformation Church, it made a great deal of difference to the history of the human Christ, and probably to the history of the European family as well.

As Christ in becoming human had acquired a human family, so he had acquired human friends. The saints, in the last medieval centuries, were rather God's extensive affinity than the model and nucleus of the universal community of the redeemed. Their lives were commemorated in the annual cycle of the liturgy, and recorded in the *Golden Legend*, which served as a handbook to it. They were, to a degree never equalled before or since, the theme of the image-maker, in paint, wood, stone and glass. Their multiplicity demonstrated that there were various ways to the friendship of God. There were those whom during his lifetime Christ had chosen, the apostles (half of whom were his relations anyway), Mary Magdalene, St Martha, St Paul. There were those who after his death had acquired his friendship by merit, the white-robed army of martyrs whose sufferings imitated those of his Passion, earned their own recompense and might transmit it to others. To such figures from a distant past had been added those who in more recognisable times had suffered at the hands of bad kings (like Thomas of Canterbury), enraged heretics (like the scourge of the Cathars, the inquisitor Peter Martyr) or Jews. There were, and continued to be, those whose capacity to rise above the human condition and make manifest God's presence in the world marked them out as saints during their lifetimes (St Catherine of Siena, the theologian of love who had brought the pope back from Avignon to Rome, the preacher San Bernardino, the doctor St Roch). There were also, like St Martin, relics of that earlier age of Western sanctity described by Peter Brown, and other figures of power like St Michael the archangel.

Yet, unlike the saints of sterner times, the corpus of God's human friendship in the last medieval century or so does not seem to be characterised, in a primary way, by the possession of power; nor do the multiplying relations formed by these saints with the rest of the Christian community seem to be in quite the same sense relations of dependence. True, one could find aggressive saints like St Antony, who was known to burn up doubters with fire, or at a homelier level St Wilgefort, known in England as the Maid

Uncumber, whose witness to virginity took the form of disembarrassing wives of their husbands. Retaliation against saints who had failed to show due power was not unknown. Relations of fear, compulsion or conflict were no doubt more common than one would deduce from the humane iconography of the period; but they seem a declining quantity, as indeed does the wonder-working power in general, though it was artificially maintained by the process of canonisation. The habit, now general, of naming children by saints seems to testify that a different relationship was envisaged: however one might conceive the relations between saints and collectivities, for the individual the name-saint was not so much a *patronus* as a *patrinus*, or superior godparent, somebody you could talk to, as Joan of Arc did, or visit at their shrine as a relative.

Hence of two possible roads to sanctity among the living, the age seems to have preferred the more benign. Although, for the average Christian, penitential hardship and self-denial were still felt to be the royal road to merit, they do not seem to have been thought much of a qualification for the status of a publicly recognised saint. The more congenial dogma about saints was that friendship with God was to be demonstrated by the furtherance of friendship among men. Among the living, like the Tuscan Bernardino or his Catalan model Vicent Ferrer, it was illustrated by their power to bring about the reconciliation of enmities, to induce powerful, if temporary, states of amity and concord in such faction-ridden cities as Siena and Barcelona; or, like St Roch, by their heroic determination to maintain the bond of charity with victims of the plague. Among dead saints it was evidenced by their patronage of the innumerable collectivities of fraternity, craft, college, parish, city, country, religious house or order of which Christendom was composed. There was certainly a problem in making the distribution of the saints conform so exactly to the distribution of the community of the living. The saints might come to act as channels for God's favour and friendship not according to merit but according to their affections, and so become enemies of one another as the angels had done before them. The problem was met in some degree by the institution of the feast of All Saints, a concept whose utility the compiler of the *Golden Legend* felt obliged to explain at some length. In the normal course of his life the Christian probably had little use for it, and it is significant that the feast was placed immediately before that of All Souls, since it was at his death-bed that the glorious company of heaven figured as the transcendental society into which he might hope to be admitted, not by his own merits but by theirs. The prospect, though earnestly prayed for, was no doubt difficult to imagine, and possibly rather daunting. It was easier, by concentrating on the individual saints and their everyday traffic between heaven and earth, to get a glimpse of what would remain a familiar social universe, but transfigured into friendship with God and with man.

If this seems an over-sentimental reading of the saints, even for a sentimental age, think of the force which was felt to lie in the following line of thought. The friend of God was the friend of man, and vice versa. Dogs, though prone to envy, were frequently friends of man. There was the dog in the legend of St Roch which told how, when the saint had finally caught the plague out of devotion to those who suffered from it, he went out into the forest and lay down to die. The dog fetched him food every day and saved his life, so earning himself a niche in the iconography of one of the most popular of saints. By contrast the people of St Roch's home town of Montpellier, when he got back there, threw him into jail, where he died. How could it be denied that such a friend of man might also be a friend of God? Hence the cult of St Guinefort, dog and martyr, dear to the people of the Lyonnais in the thirteenth century and after. Hero of a widely appreciated story, he had defended his master's baby from the attack of a venomous snake, and himself been killed by the father, who coming back to find a blood-boltered dog and an upturned cradle had assumed that he had killed the baby. God would certainly canonise him, people thought, even if the pope would not, and mothers brought weak babies to his burial-place to be cured. They would have agreed with the moral of both tales, that a dog might be a better friend to man than other men; and, if they had been familiar with this meaning of the word, with the anthropologist's view that 'religion' means the extension of social relations beyond the frontiers of merely human society.

2 Kith and Kin

(i) Baptism

The classic rite of passage of the early Church presented certain inconveniences when enacted over infants a millennium later, but the resources of Christian symbolism, official and unofficial, had kept its vigour unimpaired. Divided by a passage over the threshold of church or baptistery, what Arnold van Gennep called its rites of separation and incorporation were equally objects of intense concern. The first, or 'catechism', was a potent rite of exorcism, when the priest called on the redemptive power bequeathed by Christ to his Church to expel the Devil from a child, shattering the grasp he had acquired over men at the Fall and maintained from generation to generation: 'I exorcise thee, unclean spirit . . . , accursed one, damned and to be damned . . . '. The language of the rite, incomprehensible as it might be to the ordinary man, had nevertheless inspired a general opinion that the state of original sin was akin to that of one bewitched, whence the child should be freed as swiftly as possible, and if necessary after death, by the performance of the expelling rite. Anyone could baptise, but only the priest could effectually curse: racing death to rescue their children from the Devil, fifteenth-century Flemings tramped and waded through the night to drag warm priests from their beds. The conviction was probably growing more intense, and was stronger in northern Europe than in the south, where the unbaptised child was thought of more as a heathen or Turk than as a thing possessed, and tomorrow would usually do. It explains why people thought baptism had health-giving powers.

Exorcised at the church door, the child was then carried inside for baptism itself. This was perhaps more commonly done by sprinkling on the forehead than by the dipping face-downwards in the font which the rituals prescribed, though people seem often to have preferred the more dramatic form. Its decay probably had an effect of assimilating the act to the preceding exorcism, and of identifying the final admission of the child into the Church with his passage from the hands of the priest into those of the godparents who, as the phrase went, 'raised him from the holy font'. In the late medieval centuries the history of the incorporation of children into the community of Christians is a history of godparenthood. The characteristics of this much-appreciated institution were a tribute to the vigour and elegance of symbolic lay theology; they testified to a determination to make sure that on the other side of the waters of baptism the child would find itself received by a Christian kindred or gossip (god-sib) adequate to replace the natural kindred from which he had passed by the rites of regeneration, since flesh and blood could not inherit the kingdom of God. It was a kin-relation, it excluded natural parents, it was plural, indeed aggressively so, usually bilateral in gender and extremely various in the disparities of age involved. It restored to the child his natural relationships through the principle of *compaternitas*, which affirmed that a godparent became kin not only to the child, but to his natural family as well; the importance of this principle is evident from the use in several languages of variants of *compaternitas* to describe godparenthood in general. It created a bar to marriage between all those whom it related.

It was the purpose of the baptismal feast, with which the rites of baptism would normally conclude, to celebrate the affinity or cousinage so created, and when the clergy were not trying to restrain the multiplication of godparents they were complaining about the conduct of baptismal feasts. Of the two obligatory actions which constituted the essence of the baptismal feast, a bringing of gifts by the godparents and a participation in food and drink, they concentrated their fire on the gifts, showing themselves a good deal more sensitive to their material than to their symbolic content. It is difficult to know whether they were mainly right or wrong, but they were obviously faced with social instincts of peculiar intensity, which were understood by those who followed them to be eminently Christian, whatever the clergy or later historians might say.

Gifts and festivals symbolised friendship, and the creation of formal friendship by compaternity was the principal object of the choice of godparents in the late medieval West, as it has been in the twentieth-century Mediterranean world. The English thought the

Irish chose wolves as godparents since the friendship so created would oblige the wolf to do them no harm, which is as interesting if they were mistaken as if they were right. It points to the network of social amenities, extending from the baptism rite itself to the pleasures of backyard gossip, which can be observed among the inhabitants of Montaillou in the fourteenth century or Joan of Arc's Domrémy in the fifteenth. I doubt if it made much difference that godparents were frequently, perhaps usually, kin already: a particularly hardline council in late sixteenth-century France prohibited this, but others encouraged it as helpful in limiting matrimonial complications. To judge by modern practice, the second relation superseded the first (as in forms of address) so, one might hope, converting an often tense kinship into friendship. Godparenthood was useful in the cultivation of affinity or relations by marriage, though complex bilateral systems, starting with two grandparents for the first child, were probably an effect of the Counter-Reformation, which reduced the officially acceptable number of godparents from three to two. A sacred and specifically Christian relationship, imposing higher standards of mutual conduct on those whom it bound, representing an ideal to which natural kinship aspired but did not necessarily attain, godparenthood was so obviously a good thing that people felt confident in flouting, well into the seventeenth century, attempts to restrict or control it.

In taking a dim view of baptismal gifts, the Church seems to have been supposing that the choice of godparents was dominated by the ambition of secular advancement for children, and historians have sometimes placed godparenthood among the systems of social patronage characteristic of the later medieval West. Though this has been true in other regions or epochs of Christianity—the Orthodox Balkans, Latin America after the Spanish conquest—it does not seem to have been true of this one: *compaternitas* in the West has usually been an egalitarian relationship binding people of roughly similar standing. An exception should be made for the nobility, if only because of the prevalence here and there among them of the self-consciously pious practice of picking for godparents two poor people chosen at random. Michel de Montaigne's father, who did this for his son in 1533, told him that his motive was to persuade him to look rather towards those who held out their hands to him, than towards those who turned their backs on him. The opposite was presumably the normal case. The rest of the population seems to have been entitled to believe that their behaviour was quite as Christian as what the clergy was recommending to them, and carried on regardless.

They were perfectly capable of being persuaded of the opposite, and of altering their habits accordingly, as they did over Christian names. It was not, in principle or in historic practice, the function of baptism to name the child: the formula did not include a name, and the priest had simply to enquire what it already was. The name was therefore part of the natural endowment of the child, patronymic or descriptive, and not a Christian name as such. By the thirteenth century this was beginning to seem unsatisfactory: in northern Europe especially, the baptismal exorcism came to be felt the appropriate moment for naming, which became accordingly the function of the godparents, not of the natural parents. The original pressure for the Christianisation of names does not seem to have come from the clergy; but once naming had entered the baptismal rite, they found themselves in a position to legislate about names. A saint's name began to be required. Opposition was evidently expected: according to the later Roman Ritual, if the godparents insisted on another name, the priest was to join to it a saint's name in his register. This may look like an invasion of the rights of godparents. In fact, the humanisation of the saints at the close of the Middle Ages produced rather the contrary effect, adding the name-saint to the roll of godparents and so enhancing rather than diminishing their status. 'Christ is our principal godfather', said *Dives and Pauper*, a fifteenth-century English exposition of the Commandments.[2] Naming by saints was more obviously at odds with older systems of replicating the natural family through time, but here too accommodation was the norm. The rise of the surname, a concession in the first instance to the convenience of landlords, tax-collectors and secular authorities in general, had also the effect of providing adequately for the claims of nature: it was notably backward in Italian cities like Florence, where systems of patrilineal naming retained their force into the sixteenth century. By that date, in any case, there can have been few lineages where the saint's name was an intruder. True, the Roman Ritual implied that bizarre, obscene or ludicrous names were still being proposed in the early seventeenth century. But altogether it looks as if there was very little opposition to what was

after all a fairly fundamental change: without any general legislation on the subject, the saint's name had become more or less
universal by the Reformation. The general opinion, it seems clear,
was that in this case the injunction was a godly one, and that good
Christians would cheerfully comply with it.

Neither resistance nor compliance seems quite the word for the
state of feelings about the obligation of continence attaching to
godparenthood and compaternity. An incest barrier was obviously
requisite if baptism was to create true kinship; it was appropriate to
the sacred character of godparenthood, and a necessary condition
of the uninhibited intimacy entailed by ritual friendship. In
modern times it has been highly valued as such, and one may cite
evidence that it was so valued before the Reformation. On the other
hand, its vulnerability was the theme of Italian stories from
Boccaccio to Machiavelli, and undoubtedly also a fact of real life.
More pertinent still is the suggestion of Church statutes, as in their
own city of Florence in 1517, that familiar consort between a young
godparent and a child of the opposite sex might be expected to lead
to marriage between them, and that parents frequently made their
choice with this in mind. This has also been the burden of much
proverbial wisdom displayed at baptismal feasts, and is the simplest explanation for that implausible cliché of ecclesiastical legislation, the couple who married having forgotten that they were
related by baptismal kinship. It does seem likely that in these
specific circumstances the inhibition was often consciously
breached: considering the proliferation of sacred relationships
arising from an untoward conjunction of ideals and practice,
matrimony might well have become almost impossible otherwise.
But one would, I think, be missing something important if one
were to conclude that the prohibition had no real force. For, to set
beside the stories of its breach, there are equally well-thumbed
tales of how it was taken advantage of by those for whom continence appeared a blessing—the husband looking for a way out of
the conjugal debt standing in disguise as godparent to his child, the
forgetful couples just mentioned suddenly remembering in time to
apply for divorce. The incest barrier around the baptismal
cousinage was evidently appreciated for its high productivity in
jokes, and he would be a poor observer who supposed this pleasure
incompatible with a proper respect for a godly institution. On this
point neither Luther, who abolished it as a nuisance invented by

canon lawyers, nor the Catholic hierarchy which invented the baptismal register in order to enforce it properly, seems as reliable a guide as G. K. Chesterton, who thought that jokes were of the essence of Christianity. There was a genuine air of gaiety about the social practice of baptism at the close of the Middle Ages, a liberty entirely appropriate to the event.

(ii) Marriage

Marriage was by comparison a serious matter, in which a long-term drift towards the sacred competed with the irreducible profanities of sexuality and inheritance. There was also in this area a pre-existing corpus of ritual law and practice—Roman, Germanic or Celtic—whose relation to Christianity was debatable. In consequence the matrimonial practice of the later Middle Ages may seem confused and incoherent, as it did to many in the sixteenth century, who also thought that the Church had devoted undue attention to the subject. If, however, one looks beyond the lecture courses of celibate theologians one may find governing the matrimonial arrangements of the West between Giotto's portrayal of Anne and Joachim and the divorce of Henry VIII a sort of tradition or consensus capable of accommodating clerical idealism and the desire of the laity to behave as Christians, while balancing the requirements of the sacred and the profane.

The primary expression of the tradition was an extensive theory of incest. After experimenting unsuccessfully with something even wider the Church had since 1215 adopted, besides the prohibitions arising from baptismal relationship, the barrier of four degrees in consanguinity and a similar barrier in affinity, or relationship created by a completed sexual relation, marital or not. The further impediment of public honesty was an elaboration of the impediment of affinity which attributed to an unconsummated espousal the same prohibitive effect as a sexual relation. The doctrine was by and large accepted by the population of Europe from the thirteenth century to the sixteenth, but not because it expressed a set of instinctual or primitive taboos: people were perfectly capable of complaining, as they did in Montaillou, that marriage to one's natural kin was both more attractive in itself and a better preservative of inheritances than the exogamy the Church required. Its most characteristic feature, the theory of affinity, was in conflict

with numerous historic matrimonial systems, from that of the Jews
to that of the Irish. It was accepted, because people recognised it as
godly on grounds which had been stated by St Augustine a
millennium before. These were that the law of charity obliged
Christians to seek in marriage an alliance with those to whom the
natural ties of consanguinity did not bind them, so that the bonds
of relationship and affection might be extended through the
community of Christians: the sexual relation was to be legitimated
by the social relation it created. The form in which the doctrine was
normally now held was that marriage alliance was the pre-eminent
method of bringing peace and reconciliation to the feuds of families
and parties, the wars of princes, and the lawsuits of peasants. What
one may call the Romeo-and-Juliet theory of marriage, except that
it normally implied the subordination of the wishes of children to
the decisions of parents and the general good, was scarcely formulated in the writings of the learned until sixteenth-century critics
obliged them to think about it. But it had always been embodied in
the unspectacular workings of the Church, in the village priest
enquiring about impediments and the Court of Rome dispensing
from them. In the consciousness of the average soul it was
embedded in the social rites of marriage alliance, which
customarily proceeded from the dispatch of a 'mean person' or go-
between to open negotiations, through the introduction of the
couple to one another, the family accord concerning gifts,
inheritance and a dowry signed and sealed with a betrothal, to the
distribution of places in the wedding procession and the concluding wedding feast. For the poor and friendless this must have been
a spartan occasion, but for most people the celebration of new
kinship called for something in the style immortalised by Pieter
Bruegel: 'an honest and convenient repast', in the words of an
English spousal agreement of 1547, to be provided by the father of
the bride 'the day of the solemnisation of the said espousals or
marriage, with lodging, meat and drink for the allies, friends and
kinsfolks' of the groom and his father.[3] If we are tempted to take
such rites for granted we should remember their importance in the
relations of princes and the hostility frequently expressed towards
them in the legislation of cities, which in Italy or the Netherlands
sought to limit their consequences by restricting attendance to
immediate kin. We should also be alive to the constant possibility,
now rarely realised outside Italy until the Wars of Religion reac-

tivated it, that the process might misfire and end in a blood-bath.

The idea of marriage as alliance was also embedded in the rites of the Church, which in their intricate stratification and considerable local variety represent a kind of museum of the history of marriage. In most regions of Christendom they took place, like the first part of the baptism rite, at the church door, in German lands commonly at a special door constructed in the side of the church for this purpose. Standing upon his threshold, the priest was not enacting or administering a sacrament, but verifying the proper conduct of a social operation which embodied much profane matter but was none the less Christian and indeed sacramental without his presence. The central rite of spousals consisted of an exchange in which the father or 'friends' of the bride gave her to the groom in exchange for a symbolic counter-gift, known in France as the *arrhes* and in England as the *wed*, including the ring which he placed on her finger in token of alliance. This formula of objective exchange, in English *wedding*, which had both Roman and German ancestors and was for canon lawyers the act constitutive of marriage, had survived a variety of historic modifications tending to enlarge the individual participation of the partners and in particular to ensure that the girl was not treated as a chattel. The priest had taken the place of the father of the groom; the wife-buying aspect (prophetic of the transfer of footballers) had been toned down as antique bride-wealth (the substantive gift *to* the father of the bride) had evolved into modern dowry (the substantive gift *from* the father of the bride). In many regions, though not in England, the one-sided *datio corporis* or giving of the body had changed into a bilateral *datio corporum* (bodies) made by the parties to each other. The words of mutual troth-plight, identical for husband and wife, framed in the English rites in the memorable alliterative couplets which have (more or less) survived, and considered by theologians the essence of the sacrament, had been inserted. Nevertheless the structure of gift and counter-gift, making alliance by exchange, remained in place underneath; the arrangement was sealed by a handfast between the couple—the priest according to local custom intervening or not (not in England until the Reformation) to join their hands—and the kiss of peace. In practice the kiss was exchanged more widely among the participants at the church door, though according to the liturgy it was to be postponed to the more strictly sacred context of the *Pax* at a subsequent mass inside the church itself, and the kiss of spouses distinguished from the kiss of the congregation.

Of this social operation, at once secular and sacred, the priest was an important but not a necessary part. It could be properly accomplished without him, and if completed by sexual relations created, in the theory of the canonists and in widely observed practice, a lawful and sacramental marriage. In the role of go-between, which a conscientious priest would feel an important part of his duties, he had customary competitors; his role as public witness to the due performance of the rite could be performed by a notary and was commonly so performed in Italy. Certainly only a priest could say a nuptial mass; but this was an optional extra, except apparently in Spain. Yet his participation in the business of getting married, both liturgical and juridical, was becoming more central in the last two centuries of the Middle Ages, in Italy and elsewhere.

There were two reasons for this. The first was that, as in the case of baptism, an increasing fear of diabolic intervention—again probably stronger among northern populations than among southerners—inspired a mounting pressure for his services in the blessing of the ring, the couple and the marriage bed. The principal form taken by this intervention, known in France as the *aiguillette*, involved the knotting by a malevolent participant at the appropriate point in the marriage rite of a sort of shoelace; by the power of the Devil, to which the sexual organs were especially vulnerable, this anti-ring would ensure the failure of intercourse between the spouses and divert the process of social amity into recrimination, hostility and adultery. Fear of this and similar acts encouraged resort to the *benedictio thalami*, a rite of blessing over the couple on their first entrance into the marriage bed, of the bed itself and the bridal chamber, which had been available in most Western liturgies since the eleventh century. In the fifteenth century it became established in Germany, and it flourished in a particularly elaborate form in Scandinavia, though not apparently in England. In the south of France fear of the *aiguillette* was thought to discourage people from marrying in church: but since the priest was unlikely to attend the wedding feast and to join the pair when they retired to bed unless the company had come to church beforehand, the effect of such fears was to multiply his interventions in the liturgy. The ring, now blessed immediately before being placed on the bride's finger, became a talisman of fidelity and perhaps of fertility, as well as a symbol of social alliance: an object whose mystic endowments inspired the godly in sixteenth-century England to seek, with little success, to ban it from the marriage rite. Spousals unblessed began to appear as risky a prospect as a child unexorcised.

The second reason for the enlargement of the priest's role was a paradoxical consequence of the doctrine maintained by theologians since the twelfth century that an exchange of consent and appropriate words between two physically qualified individuals in any circumstances whatever constituted a sacramental marriage. Its chief effect was to make marriage possible without the participation or consent of parents or the sequence of social rites. It is a tribute to the general understanding of relatively abstruse points of canon law that the doctrine was widely taken advantage of by young people whose mutual attraction was frustrated by their families, and by young men looking for a way of persuading girls to let themselves be seduced. The motives for the doctrine were understandable, involving the free availability of sacramental grace and the right of children to follow a religious or ecclesiastical vocation against their parents' opposition; but it was an example of the feeble hold of scholastic theologians, as against canon lawyers, on the idea that the sacraments were social institutions. It is fairly clear from the records of Church courts that the doctrine had inserted into the marriage law of Christendom a large element of anarchic confusion, and aroused very widespread hostility among the respectable laity, who regarded it as a seducer's charter. No doubt their principal motive was the defence and enlargement of inheritances, but they were also defending the unwritten tradition of marriage as a process of Christian alliance against what seemed inconceivable dereliction on the part of the Church. Marriage, clandestine or not, entailed for them all sorts of binding relationships; where these were not entered into with due consideration and proper process and sanctified by the appropriate rites, they would institutionalise not amity but ill will. There was another problem. Clandestine marriage might seem to keep the priest at an even greater distance from the marriage process than did the customary arrangements, but in practice, especially in regions like Italy where the role of the priest in these arrangements was modest, the opposite was often the case. Couples genuinely seeking to marry without parental consent were likely, like Romeo and Juliet, to seek the witness of a priest; hence clandestine marriage (the Church could not regard such marriages as clandestine, but common opinion did) had often the effect of exacerbating the tug-of-war concealed in the marriage rites between the father and the priest.

Legislation on the subject would have been required in any case, if not from the Church, then from secular authorities like the extremely Catholic government of Henri II of France, which in 1556 declared clandestine marriage, by which it meant a marriage without parental consent, a criminal offence entailing the obligatory disinheritance of the parties. The edict may be regarded as a defence of the unwritten tradition, though in a distinctively patriarchal version appropriate to sixteenth-century feelings. It clearly influenced the tone of French pastoral advice on the subject. For the Church, legislation had become urgent as soon as Luther had denied that marriage was a sacrament, meaning on the one hand that the Augustinian tradition was misconceived, that impediments should be minimal and that the clergy should not meddle with the law of marriage at all; and on the other that parental consent should be obligatory and clandestine marriage invalid. This put the Fathers of the Council of Trent, assembled in defence of Catholicism in 1563, in a grave dilemma. How were they to condemn Luther, and to defend the Augustinian tradition and the sacramentality of marriage, while conceding to the demands of Catholic parents enough to prevent their exasperation driving them *en bloc* to the reformers, as it seemed to be doing in France? Led by the Cardinal of Lorraine, French, Iberian and some Italian bishops demanded the invalidation of clandestine marriages; a rather smaller but equally intransigent body of Italians, supported by the papacy, replied that the defence of the Catholic theology of the sacraments, and the urgency of condemning Luther's surrender of marriage to the secular authorities, made this absolutely out of the question. Since almost nobody was prepared to defend the view that mere puberty was an adequate condition for marrying without parental consent, it proved possible to agree on an age below which lack of parental consent would render a marriage invalid, though the compromise (20 for men, 18 for women) was more favourable to the Italians than the French, who were looking for something nearer their monarchy's enactment of 30 and 25.

What to do about those above that age who should contract marriages without publicity, which for most participants meant marrying without the consent of parents and the social rites, provoked a hopeless deadlock.

At his wits' end, the principal legate, Cardinal Morone, came up with something which deserves a prominent place in the annals of chairmanship. He proposed in effect to accept the demand that clandestine marriages be invalidated, but to alter the definition of clandestinity. In future, all marriages were to be contracted in the face of the Church before the *parish* priest and witnesses, after the publication of three banns; the priest would enter them in a register. All other marriages, private or public, performed before any other priest or person, were to be null and void. Couples were exhorted, but not required, to postpone conjugal relations until after the marriage had been blessed at a nuptial mass. The proposal was accepted, as the only way of reconciling the parties, and became law. Although it had in some ways been prefigured by the preceding history of the matter, it was a bolt from the blue, and it is unclear how far the Council was aware that it was enacting a revolution in Christianity. In sweeping away the canon law doctrine that a spousal contract followed by *copula carnis* constituted a Christian marriage, in brushing aside the vast corpus of customary rites and arrangements as having no sacramental force, it transformed marriage from a social process which the Church guaranteed to an ecclesiastical process which it administered. The implications of the decree were made explicit in the Roman Ritual of 1612, which transplanted the rite from the church door to the altar, affirmed no more than that it was 'decent' for the relatives of the couple to be present, and in general paid scant regard to the traditions of Catholic Europe, least of all in Italy. Much impeded by secular governments, civil lawyers, and loyalty to local liturgies and customs, the new regime had probably not been generally absorbed much before 1700. Important, perhaps crucial, for the character of Catholicism, the event was part of something wider. The Church of England, which retained the existing *law* of marriage until Parliament enacted an equivalent of the Tridentine system in 1753, had from the start adopted a *ritual* of marriage which bore a family resemblance to the new Roman rite in that it enhanced the role of the priest or minister and abolished the location at the church door. Most other reformed Churches, though not the Lutherans, were guided in the opposite direction by the conviction that marriage was not a sacrament but a civil contract. Hence the enactment of civil marriage by the godliest Parliament of the English Interregnum in 1653. Either way the marriage contract lost its liminal status, its precarious situation at the juncture of the sacred and the profane which had been symbolised by the transaction at the church door.

(iii) Death

In matters connected with death the pre-Reformation Church, though it had upset some of the intellectuals, had done nothing similar to upset the instincts of the laity; indeed there is a case, though not I think a very persuasive one, for saying that it had done the reverse. Multitudinous as they were, its provisions for death and the dead represented one of its major resources in the conflict against the reformers. The history of reformed countries, and especially of Germany, shows a good deal of popular insistence on maintaining as much as possible of the traditional regime, whatever difficulties this might create for reformed theologians and pastors.

In outline the rites of death were practically anti-social. As conveyed in the *commendatio animae* (bedside prayers) and the burial rite, they dealt with a soul radically separated, by death-bed confession and last will, from earthly concerns and relationships. They left him alone with the priest, fortified by prayers and blessings for the dismaying sequence of perils and ordeals which he would have to pass on his way to paradise, the consort of the saints, the glorious company of heaven. In that sense the radical individualism or self-preoccupation which Philippe Ariès has claimed to be the special characteristic of dying in the late Middle Ages was embodied in the liturgy of death. It was expressed in its most memorable invocations—'Out of the depths have I cried to thee, O Lord . . .', 'Libera me domine de morte aeterna . . .', 'Go forth on thy journey, Christian soul . . . '. And this entailed something more than the evident fact that we die alone: it had to do with the doctrine, by now established but not formally expressed in the liturgy, that the destiny of the soul was settled not at the universal Last Judgement of the *Dies Irae*, but at a particular judgement intervening immediately after death. More mundanely, it had to do with the invention of the will, liberating the individual from the constraints of kinship in the disposition of his soul, body and goods, to the advantage, by and large, of the clergy.

In practice there was a good deal more to it than that: death may be an individual event for the dying, but it is a social event for those who remain behind. While the priest made his way to the bedside, the tolling of a bell alerted the neighbours in rather the way that an ambulance siren does nowadays. There were rites of informing the neighbourhood, for laying out the body in the house, for watching (the wake), mourning and reading the will; rites for carrying the body to church; rites of the funeral properly speaking, the office of the dead performed over the body placed before the altar; rites of burial; funeral baked-meats; obligations to be fulfilled towards the soul, commemorations and anniversaries individual and collective. This most elaborate structure, which was at the close of the Middle Ages in a state of rapid enlargement, represented some kind of a compromise between divergent pieties, and between *pietas* itself in the proper sense (that is, family duty) and the bare skeleton of the liturgy. The natural religion of kinship and friendship, which the Church on the whole managed to keep at a distance from the bedside itself, entered into its element once the soul had departed from the body. It was certainly unusual, though it happened in Corsica, for the body thereafter to remain permanently within the family precincts; but until its departure for the churchyard it remained in the possession of its living kin, and the custom seems more or less universal that this period must include at least a single night. There was indeed in Flanders, and no doubt elsewhere, a good deal of Church legislation which required the body to be transferred immediately after death to church or churchyard, but it was probably ignored. There was a domestic ritual of laying out the body to be performed, and such acts as the clipping of hair and nails to maintain the presence of the dead person in the house and prevent them from getting into the hands of malicious persons, of which we have an account from Montaillou. There were rites of lamentation, usually done by women—as by Mary at the cross —which often entailed, especially in wilder parts like Corsica, passionate denunciations and demands for vengeance on any who might be held responsible for the death. There was, again probably universal but most elaborate among the Irish, for whom it has often seemed to be the principal obligation of religion, the wake. This highly structured event, doubtless of ancient origins, featured the corpse, the family, friends and professional mourners, and proceeded from weeping and wailing, through joke and insult (from which in extreme cases the corpse might be expected to arise in wrath), to a display by the survivors of recovered aggressive and sexual powers. The wake was certainly no joke as far as the Church was concerned: prohibition having failed, it had encouraged, and in some regions (like England) required, the funeral as a substitute, the corpse lying before the altar rather than the domestic hearth. To get the body into its hands it was prepared to tolerate, above all for the nobility, displays of family arrogance in church a good deal beyond what would have been acceptable on other occasions. Resistance to such self-indulgence by the stipulation of a poor funeral was, as in the choice of godparents, the mark of a pious will.

The principal religious attraction of the funeral rite was that it included the mass for the dead and so enabled the bereaved to launch in a decent way the process of fulfilling their obligations to the soul of the departed, as distinguished from his body. Why the mass for the dead had come to be the great vehicle of Christian feelings which it had become by the fifteenth century is something we shall explore in a moment. Beginning in the monasteries of the early Middle Ages, it had become an independent activity of the wealthy laity by the thirteenth century, and thereafter diffused itself steadily through the rest of the population. There is little reason to suppose that by the Reformation it was less practised by one sector of the population than by another, though since a quantitative view of the efficacy of such masses had become established and priests had to be paid for saying them, the impressiveness of people's investment in them would vary according to their income. From the fourteenth century the nobility endowed perpetual chantries, the middling sort subscribed to pious fraternities, nearly everybody provided for trentals or anniversary commemorations, the poor paid for single masses. Providing for the demand was the main or sole activity of a large and increasing number of priests.

Although a good deal of the steam inside this massive engine was provided, as Ariès indicated, by individual panic and self-regard, most of it came from social *pietas* towards family and friends; the insertion of the mass for the dead into the social arrangements of death represented a large accommodation by the Church to the view, denied in principle by the liturgy, that the Christian dead remained part of their own kith and kin. There is an astonishing variety of evidence to the fact: inscriptions in chantry chapels, the terms of endowments, the discussions of theologians, the hymns of Breton peasants, Provençal contracts of *affreramentum* or house-sharing, German contracts of marriage. It was, we shall see, in the nature of the mass for the dead to offer an outlet to such familial piety. Hence, to give an unusually comprehensive example, the terms of a chantry foundation of an English gentleman dating from about 1500, which required the simple 'May they rest in peace', which concluded the mass for the dead, to be elaborated as follows: 'May the souls of the kings of England, of William Whaplode (founder), his father, his mother, brothers, sisters, wives, blood-relations, friends and benefactors rest in peace. Amen.'[4] It was, after all, the friends and relations who would have to carry the can if something went wrong in the process of death, and the dead, unable to rest in peace, returned to them as ghosts. Unlike the modern ghost, the traditional ghost was personal not real; he haunted people not places and demanded the fulfilment of obligations towards him from those whose duty it was to fulfil them. The law applied universally, to peasant-girls as to princes of Denmark. What a ghost normally required was the saying of an adequate number of masses to ensure the salvation of his soul, or the execution of some provision of his will whose neglect had upset the accommodation with the Almighty which he had reached on his death-bed; he also fairly often required the avenging of his murder. He was in short an embodiment of familial piety. The seventeenth-century English Catholic theologian Thomas White, who held that ghost stories arose 'from the frequent cogitation and passionate affection of the living towards their departed friends', seems to have got to the heart of the matter, though fear and guilt were doubtless important as well. It has been suggested that a belief in ghosts underlies late medieval religious feelings to a degree which puts them outside Christianity properly speaking. This surely rather overdoes the importance of the matter, and seems an unfaithful description of the frame of mind of people who here, as in baptism and marriage, were trying to be decent Christians. Here too they seem entitled to their belief that natural pieties were by and large compatible with Christianity; but in pursuing them they certainly made a great deal of difference to the tradition of Christian dying.

Between the other-worldliness of the liturgical texts and the natural emotions of those who paid for them to be said, there was a middle region which sustained some of the most characteristic expressions of Catholic piety towards the dead. It had been opened up by developments in the theology of life after death, and in the practice of burial: together they had made it possible to envisage the dead as having passed, not into an unapproachable community of the saints, but into what has been called an 'age group' of the population, whose relations with the living could be put on a manageable collective footing. The doctrine of purgatory had been creeping up on Western Christendom since the early Middle Ages. It affirmed that besides the traditional heaven and hell there was a third region of the other world, an intermediate destination where most of those who were ultimately destined for the company of heaven would have in the meantime to undergo due punishment for their sins. It was a fairly evident application of Anselm's rule of satisfaction, the more convincing as the ancient penitential machinery for enforcing satisfaction in this world had fallen into decay. In defining the doctrine in a steadily more explicit form, as it did in the Councils of Lyon (1274), Florence (1439) and Trent, the Church seems to have been as much following as determining the simple deductions of lay instinct and speculation. Dante's *Divine Comedy*, which had after 1320 put purgatory indelibly on the map of Western consciousness, was a monument to both its learned and its instinctual sources. This did not mean that the average person now had a clear view of the kind of place, or rather state, that purgatory was. The idea, not recognised by Dante but favoured by the Church on quasi-scriptural grounds, that the agent of purgation was fire and purgatory a sort of cave from which, in the end, souls would fly up to heaven does not seem to have impinged much on the general consciousness until the fifteenth century. Thereafter, encouraged by the indulgence preachers, it made a great deal of headway.

Meanwhile the common-sense view was that the souls of the dead would naturally be more or less where their bodies were, in the churchyard, and suffering rather from cold and wet than from excessive heat. The conviction transpires from the discussions of the subject which occurred in Montaillou, from a vast corpus of

folk-tales, and indeed from a certain amount of respectable liturgical practice. The falling back on purgatory as the immediate
destination of the dead made it possible to envisage death as a
passage into a collectivity whose location was the churchyard, and
which therefore possessed its own proper segment of the common
territory, as the living possessed theirs. The medieval churchyard,
as Ariès has explained, was a social institution of distinctive
character. The early Christians, conforming to the pattern still
expressed in the liturgy, had buried their dead *ad sanctos*, close to
the tombs of the martyrs and outside inhabited places. With
regional exceptions, like Ireland, the medieval burial-place was
commonly in the middle of the dwelling-places of the living, in a
churchyard which was also a centre of social activity, a place for
festivity and trade. Consecrated, a holy place, it was an area of
inviolability, a sanctuary or *Friedhof* which would be polluted by
the shedding of blood or seed and require reconsecration. In
passing into the community of the dead one was passing into a
region of compulsory peace, and it was in this way that the
detachment of the dying from their relationships among the living
could be understood and to a degree accepted. The churchyard was
a collective place: individual burial-places were not marked or
remembered, and when the flesh had rotted the bones were
commonly, like Yorick's, dug up and added to the anonymous
mass in the charnel-house.

During the fifteenth century, representations of the community
of the dead as a model for the community of the living achieved a
memorable form in the *danse macabre, Totentanz* or dance of the
dead (not 'dance of death' until the theme was taken up by
sixteenth-century artists who did not quite see the point). Painted
on the cloister wall of a number of celebrated churchyards, notably
of the Cimetière des Innocents in Paris, it portrayed a circle where
the dead alternate, holding hands, with the living, and lead them in
a dance around the graves. The skeletal dead, an undifferentiated
community of equals, dance keenly, the living reluctantly:
weighed down by robes, possessions and thoughts about status,
they have to be dragged in by the dead, polite but firm. The grave
in the fifteenth century was not a private but a public place and
embracing, of a sort, compulsory.

The dead as a model for the living, and death as a passage into
collective existence, impinged on the life of communities at at least

two moments. When John Donne advised his Jacobean hearers not to ask for whom the bell tolled, since it tolled for them, he was invoking a complex of formal practice and customary behaviour which affirmed that when an individual died the normal distinctions within a community were suspended. At the tolling of the bell the neighbourhood was encouraged to drop what it was doing and follow the priest to the bedside, or at least to say a prayer for the soul of the dying; indulgences were granted for attendance at death-bed and funeral procession. By the fifteenth century it was very likely that the business of carrying the body to church, of seeing to its burial, even of watching by the body in the house, would be in the hands of a parish fraternity dedicated, like lifeboatmen, to that charitable purpose. The general responsiveness to these invitations to collective piety is evident from a variety of customs exemplifying what has been called the 'truce of death'. Since the confession and, if relevant, will of the dying had to include a granting of forgiveness to offenders and a seeking for forgiveness for offences, it was possible for those at enmity with the dying to appear at death-bed and burial rites; the stereotype of the death-bed reconciliation is something more than a cliché. There was also the rule, widely observed later, that the *nuntius mortis*, the person who would go round to give formal notice of the death, must not be related to, or even friends with, the dead person. Such obligatory togetherness has ended, in modern times, with the funeral feast after burial. It existed also in the general feast of All Souls, which was one of the great festivals of traditional Christianity, drawing its strength from an increasing concern in the Church and among the pious about the release from purgatory of those who had no or insufficient living 'friends' to pray or have masses said for them.

The evidence for this concern is widespread in the prayers and rites, in the wills of individuals, the activities of parishes, and occasionally in the records of governments, of the late Middle Ages: the Christian was reminded with increasing insistence of 'all the faithful departed', those who had nobody to pray for them, all those buried in the churchyard, all the souls of the parish. On the feast itself the formal business consisted of a requiem for the souls of the parish, a procession around the churchyard, and the blessing of the graves; the task of embellishing these rituals was frequently, perhaps especially in France, the function of the burial fraternity, which might also support similar activities throughout the year. Folklore suggests how intensely the occasion was cultivated. On the vigil of All Souls in the fifteenth century, the church bells rang through the night, German children lit candles and laid cakes on the graves, or lit bonfires in the churchyard. This on the grounds that the souls, during the feast, would have a brief release from their dismal situation and come out of their graves for warmth and succour. Those who had 'friends' would naturally make for the domestic hearth, where hot metal surfaces ought to be covered so that the souls would not, being naked, burn themselves by sitting down; the rest might warm themselves and get something to eat in the churchyard. Similarly the living poor should be fed by their more fortunate neighbours. The outlines of such popular rites are still visible in the rites of Hallowe'en, moved forward by a night presumably at the instance of reforming authorities anxious to eliminate their relation with praying for the dead. There was certainly, as Hallowe'en suggests, an element of fear concealed in the bell-ringing and the bonfires, and of propitiation in the gifts. But since the feast was a recent invention in a state of creative effervescence, it is difficult to see it, as Keith Thomas has suggested, as preaching the submission of the living to ancestral ways imposed by an implacable gerontocracy of the dead. The dead may have been bad-tempered, jealous of the living, prone to play tricks; but their condition was essentially pitiable, and the message of All Souls a message of charity towards them.

Until, and probably in practice for a good while after, the Reformation, the churchyard remained a scene of collective rites, the home of a sector of the population collectivised by the process of dying. Yet the sense of family property in the dead was ultimately ineradicable. Sustained by freedom of choice in burial, by continuing belief in the ultimate primacy of family obligation, by the necessities of the clergy in the aftermath of war, and no doubt by the decline of agricultural collectivism, it was in the process of organising its revenge. In the long run, it would achieve, in both reformed and Catholic regions, a sort of enclosure movement in the territory of the dead, destined to accommodate the claims of family ownership. By the Reformation, without having made much impression on the churchyard itself, it had made a considerable difference to the inside of churches, as evidence of family possessiveness accumulated under floors, in chapels, on pillars and walls. The Council of Basel complained in 1432 that incumbents, in search of an honest penny, were sullying the churches and turning them into cemeteries. The carving up of the churchyard into a set of family allotments, like the imposition of a reverent silence and the removal of snuffling pigs, was a prospect for the future.

3 Sin and Penance

(i) Sin

In the age of Dante, Langland and Chaucer, and still in the age of Thomas More, when the Scottish poet William Dunbar wrote a poem about them, the principal vehicle of the moral tradition of the West was the doctrine of the seven deadly sins: pride, envy, anger, avarice, gluttony, sloth and lechery in that order. As a moral system the seven deadly sins were not a model of coherence, and expositors differed a good deal in their attempts to reduce them to order. Most of them, however, brought to the sequence a distinction between the spirit and the flesh, divided the sins according to whether they were diseases of one or the other, and argued that diseases of the spirit were more to be avoided than diseases of the flesh. Pride, envy and anger fell into the first category; gluttony, lechery and usually sloth into the second; avarice shifted insecurely between one and the other. So interpreted, the seven deadly sins were a system of community ethics making more excuse for the sins of concupiscence than for those of aversion. The sins of aversion destroy community, but without some flirtation with the sins of concupiscence there is unlikely to be a community at all.

This community ethics was expounded in the Lenten sermons of the pre-Reformation period by parsons, friars, and town and cathedral preachers, whose doctrine of sin may be represented, more or less, by the parson's 'tale' which concluded Chaucer's *Canterbury Tales* and was composed about 1390. For him, as for Dante, pride, envy and wrath came first. Pride was a social, not a metaphysical or Promethean, phenomenon and consisted essentially in putting the claims of degree before those of sociability. The parson recalled Dante on the social benefits of humility and the central importance of the act of greeting or salutation, but, unlike Dante, failed to convey the feeling that these were transcendental matters. He was convincing on envy, as were most of his contemporaries, whose treatment of the subject may confirm the view that envy is the characteristic vice of populations of peasants. Envy had two branches: jealousy of other men's prosperity, and pleasure in their misfortune. It implied, as Dante had explained, what has been called the doctrine of the limited good: the theory which holds that there is a fixed amount of good fortune in the world, so that what accrues to one member of a community is so much taken from the rest. It was, the parson thought, the worst of all sins, since the most directly opposite to solidarity and charity, and the source of back-biting, rancour and discord. It was related to wrath as an interior feeling to its outward expression: wrath did not really mean uncontrollable bad temper, but a settled and formal hatred towards a neighbour, inspiring acts of malice or vengeance against him. We need to understand the universal presence of wrath in the moral thinking of the later Middle Ages. It was the legitimate posture of God towards the seed of Adam, and also cultivated by the saints, though less than hitherto; the Devil, the universal fiend, was a pure embodiment of it; a wide range of human acts was thought to exemplify it. The parson's list naturally contained manslaughter, and swearing, cursing and verbal abuse; but also usury, and the refusal of wages and alms; witchcraft, conjuring and divination; contraception, onanism and abortion. As it concealed a doctrine of the limited good, this moral theory also implied that social acts were performed in a universe of friendship and enmity: love of one's enemy was the supreme Christian virtue because it was the hardest of all, and because it was the true imitation of Christ 'that died for his enemies'.

The parson did not prove a very coherent guide to concupiscence. This may have been due to a lack of experience, learning or vision on Chaucer's part, or the fault may have been more general. The sins of concupiscence were made to seem either trivial, like sloth and gluttony (mainly in drink), or really sins against solidarity, like avarice and lechery: by lechery he mainly meant adultery, which took up more space than any other sin and was ascribed principally to wives and priests. There was nothing here of the exquisite union of tenderness and severity in Dante's portrayal of Paolo and Francesca in the *Divine Comedy*: adultery was not a case of the ambiguities of love, but a particularly nasty form of theft. No doubt this was more realistic; and it would certainly have been customary for Dante to have made more of the fact that the lovers' story ended in their murder by Francesca's husband, an example of the perturbation and dissension among men which adultery was peculiarly apt to provoke. In fact the incoherence of the late medieval discussion of adultery, and of sexuality in general, seems to lie in a failure to be entirely candid about the nature of the perturbation caused: what was being presented as an offence against charity was often actually being felt as an offence against holiness. The parson's choice of language would have confirmed a general feeling that the sexual act was intrinsically shameful, like leprosy, and that its ominous influence in communities lay not so much in causing havoc in human relations, as in diffusing a pollution which would automatically bring down the wrath of God upon all. Hence the ban on marriage during Lent and at other seasons, the doctrine that sexual acts between the married were always venially sinful, the purification of women after childbirth, the peculiar preoccupation with sexuality among priests. The pollutant conception of sexuality had probably been intensified by well-intended efforts of Aristotelian theologians like Thomas Aquinas to take a naturalistic or biological view of ethics; these had the effect of much extending the concept of sins against nature while failing to make much impression on the traditional view of conventional sexual relations between the married.

This accommodation to instincts about sexual pollution must make one hesitate before accepting the idea of the seven deadly sins as an instrument for maintaining the primacy of charity. Yet whenever, for example, the ethics of sixteenth-century rural communities are investigated, as they have been in England, in Italy and elsewhere, what invariably comes to light is the feeling that charity was what mattered. The disparity of evidence does not, in my opinion, indicate a serious difference of moral judgement between the teachers and the taught, but it does seem to say something about a particular complex of moral convictions widely prevailing in the West on the eve of the Reformation. My impression is not that the average soul now thought chastity more important than charity, but that between them preachers and people had created a moral consensus dwelling by predilection on topics where the two could be seen as one: unchastity as a social offence, and uncharity as a type of the unclean. Hence, as will emerge, the growing obsession with witchcraft. Hence the last expression of moral revivalism in unreformed Christendom, the puritan commonwealth erected in Florence during the 1490s by the Dominican prophet Savonarola. Hence also the complicated mixture of outrage, disgust and anxiety which inspired the rabbling of married priests or the massacre of Protestants by embattled traditionalists during the sixteenth century.

In the mean time two things had happened which were to bring to a close the reign of the seven deadly sins as the principal vehicle of the moral tradition of the West. After a good deal of experiment by authors and preachers unsatisfied with their traditional order on the grounds that it gave the sins of concupiscence, including avarice, insufficient prominence, and of criticism by humanists who thought the whole concept barbarous, a new order was arrived at; it kept pride at the top, but promoted avarice and lechery and demoted envy and anger in the list. It was consecrated by the Catholic catechisms of the sixteenth century, and one of the reasons for its adoption was that in Latin the initial letters of the sins formed the more memorable, though meaningless, word *saligia*; it does not seem to suggest any very intelligible concept of sin. This was less important than it might have been, for the sevenfold entity had by now been relieved of the major burden of the moral conscience of Christians. It had been replaced by the Ten Commandments. For Chaucer, and indeed for Dante, these had been a high doctrine, to be left to divines; there were still in the sixteenth century quite well-informed Catholics, like the Friulian miller Menocchio, the hero of Carlo Ginzburg's *The Cheese and the Worms*, who had never heard of them. But the advent of the catechism was to confirm, on all sides of the confessional mêlée, a transition to the Ten Commandments as the moral system of the West which the teaching Church seems to have largely made in the fifteenth century. Its results may fairly be described as revolutionary.

In trying to relate this moral tradition to the facts of life during the century or so before the Reformation, we shall have, for better or worse, to do without statistics. I doubt if we can do better than proceed on the assumption that in a system of transcendental ethics there will be some positive correlation between the centrality of a precept and the frequency with which it is breached. If, that is, we take the moral tradition to be preaching, however imperfectly, the primacy of charity and the relative benignity of the sins of concupiscence, we can expect the sins of aversion to be those to which people were peculiarly inclined. There seems reasonable evidence that this was the case. They included sins which were actually regarded as virtuous or obligatory in the only alternative moral tradition in the field, which turned on the notions of honour and dishonour. This tradition supported a code of behaviour which required retaliation for offences, entered into a confusing relation with ideas of Christian provenance in the concept of chivalry, and emerged in purer form and with lasting influence in the sixteenth-century Italian ethos of the duel. It was not, at least until this point, the prerogative of the nobility, though it may be that for the rest of the population, as for women, honour and shame were more exclusively implicated in sexual matters.

The sensitivities of honour were a considerable factor in the 'tension' and 'violent tenor' of fifteenth-century life which form the subject of a famous chapter of Johan Huizinga's *The Waning of the Middle Ages*. Huizinga's may not be a name to conjure with in the history of criminality, and his specific attribution of primacy to the sins of pride and avarice may seem overdone. But there is something fundamentally persuasive about his depiction of the over-mastering power in fifteenth-century people of the passions of aversion and hostility, of a delight in hatred and vengeance against which the pleasures of concupiscence seem pale and contrived. No wonder, wrote the Burgundian chronicler Chastellain, that princes are so often at enmity with one another, 'for they are men . . . and their natures are subject to many passions such as hatred and envy, and their hearts a very sink of these, because of the pride they have in ruling'. The description would do as well for the age of Henry VIII as for that of Joan of Arc.

Vengeance among princes, party passion in cities and states, the diligent pursuit of social hostilities at every level of the pyramid of status, the universal conviction that the social and political worlds were divided into one's friends and one's enemies: these were possibly not more prevalent in actual fact than they had been in Dante's time. Perhaps they only appear so because of a multiplica-tion of legal instances or the advance of a more abstract and public view of crime. Still, no one could say that fifteenth-century moral authorities like San Bernardino, who preached the primacy of charity to the citizens of Siena, were not expounding a relevant morality.

Outside the handbooks for confessors, and the records of Church courts struggling with the modalities of the marriage contract, the chronicles of fifteenth-century concupiscence deal mainly in adultery, rape and prostitution. They suggest in the outlook of civic authorities, who represented something like a state of public opinion, a balance leaning towards togetherness and against holiness, though it differed in different places. Florence, perhaps because of its reputation as a sink of sodomy, seems to have been an unusually puritan city. It was organising adolescent continence well before Savonarola made this the spearhead of his moral revival, and was already cultivating the privacy and domesticity which generally go with it. Northern cities like Ypres, where sensibilities were less refined, offered a *de facto* tolerance to certain kinds of harmless fornication while cracking down fiercely on female adultery, but also on rape, which was extremely common and usually connected with other sorts of violence. Female adulterers were drowned and rapists hanged. Prostitution was a profession exercised in the public baths, called *étuves*, *stoven* or stews: Flanders had a reputation for its girls, and exported them to London and the south. It was not formally legal, and prostitutes and bawds might expect to be had up from time to time; but the climate was obviously more like that of twentieth-century than of Victorian London, and one may find scenes from the stews carved on the roof-beams of town halls.

By contrast with this residual shiftiness of attitude in the north, a number of southern towns took a perfectly coherent attitude to prostitution. Like the Netherlanders, they dreaded adultery and rape as the really baleful effects of lechery, and looming threats to the Christian peace of their cities; they also seem to have been confronted with a custom of collective rape by gangs of youths which was deeply entrenched in local mores. No doubt it was something to do with the concept of honour. Their conclusion was that it was their Christian duty to authorise and maintain a properly supervised system of public prostitution, additional to what was provided by the stews. Their municipal brothels were supposed not to admit young boys, married men or the clergy, and to close in Holy Week, on Sundays and some other feasts. The girls and their manageress were considered to be practising an honourable and useful profession; their behaviour seems to have been sober, even pious, and they might look forward at the end of their career to a respectable marriage and a municipal dowry, or to a decent retirement in a convent of *filles repenties*. The institution has been found during the fifteenth century from Dijon to Avignon: its decline in the middle of the sixteenth, in consequence of a series of suppressions concluded by a French royal edict of 1560, seems to mark the same kind of transition as the reordering of the seven deadly sins.

Something of the sort was evidently happening in Italian cities in the transition from the Renaissance to the Counter-Reformation, as is testified by the publication of Boccaccio, from the 1570s, in expurgated editions. Some may wonder whether *The Decameron* should be taken as a moral treatise, but Boccaccio had certainly preached that the sins of concupiscence were trivial by comparison with the sins of aversion; his rider that the Christian community would suffer more by repressing than by tolerating them was in keeping with the views of the burghers of Dijon and Avignon. Traces of it may be found in Italian pastoral practice around 1500, and in the (by then distinctly embarrassed) defence of the Roman stews put up by Catholic propagandists later in the century. But the tradition about concupiscence, still probably quite strong among the rural population, though struggling with deep if inarticulate feelings of shame, had by this time suffered a weakening of the flank which made it vulnerable to the artillery trained upon it by moralists of holiness from Savonarola to Carlo Borromeo. The civilised morality of the Italian élite in the early sixteenth century was in many ways attractive, but from the point of view of the moral tradition it had the flaw of failing to maintain its tolerance towards the flesh inside the historic structure of concern about the passions of hostility. In devaluing like several popes, or positively despising like Machiavelli, the superior claims of peace and charity, the learned and powerful of early sixteenth-century Italy showed themselves to be in something like the moral crisis which Burckhardt diagnosed in *The Civilisation of the Renaissance in Italy*.

To be fair to them, they were victims of an exterior process beyond their control. As, throughout Europe, the retaliation and regulation of offences drifted out of the field of private arrangement into the purview of the secular ruler and ultimately of the abstract State, the institutions of Christianity drifted into a position marginal to the maintenance of peace among Christians. As the peace of reconciliation gave way before the peace of tranquillity, the Church was bound to find its traditional hierarchy of values losing its grip on reality, and to look for a new one. The process took a very long time: there is no reason to agree with the opinion that by 1600 sexuality had become the central matter of Catholic ethics. But in the long run it is probably true that the Church made up on the roundabouts of concupiscence what it had lost on the swings of aversion.

(ii) Carnival

Sin required penance from the individual, as Dante had expounded it; it also, as a stain on the community of Christians, required penance from the population at large, collective ascetic rituals of which the most important was the annual season of Lent. Though generally felt to be essential to individual salvation and public prosperity, penance remained a daunting prospect: the task of persuading people to enter upon it was likened by the Strassburg preacher John Geiler to getting a horse on to a small boat. The horse might pass more readily if its steps were guided by the formalities of a rite of passage. So by the sixteenth century the moment at which the population passed from its carnal into its penitential state had become a time for the vigorously cultivated rites of separation generally known as Carnival. These were, despite some appearances, Christian in character, and they were medieval in origin: although it has been widely supposed that they continued some kind of pre-Christian cult, there is in fact no evidence that they existed much before 1200. The Italian term *carnevale* derived from the *dominica carnelevalis* or Quadragesima Sunday, the feast which in the Roman and Milanese liturgies marked for the clergy the passage from the normal to the penitential regime, and signified the abolition of meat or flesh; those words in use in other vernaculars (*antruejo/introitus, carême-entrant*) referred to the entrance into Lent. As a period of time and a moral conception Carnival was one half of an entity of which the other half was Lent. The unity-in-opposition of the pair, which seems a notable instance of the structural anthropology practised by Claude Lévi-Strauss, was the theme of the French and Spanish poems which diffused the conception in the thirteenth and fourteenth centuries, and also of a line of pictorial representations memorably concluded in the middle of the sixteenth by the *Fight between Carnival and Lent* of Pieter Bruegel.

Carnival normally occurred, and has continued to occur, as a series of three or six days ending on Shrove Tuesday or *Mardi Gras*. These were feast-days in that work was prohibited, the private became public, and communities functioned as a whole or through bodies specially created for the purpose. The object of the feast was to represent the workings of carnality in general and, out of the doings of the past year, to bring the corpus of sin to light, in order that it might be got rid of in time for Lent. Carnality was almost invariably embodied in a carnival figure who dominated the feast, was carried in procession during it, and tried, condemned and executed (usually by burning) at the end of it. In these more formal proceedings the seven sins were represented by Gluttony, just as abstinence from meat had come to represent the penitential asceticisms of Lent. Carnival was a fat man; during the feast it was obligatory to eat a great deal, especially fat things like pigs and pumpkins, and drink to match; in Nantes Shrove Tuesday was dedicated to S. Dégobillard (St Vomit), whom one may think an appropriate patron for the whole feast.

It should not be deduced from this that Carnival was more concerned with the sins of concupiscence than with those of aversion. Certainly a good deal of sexual display and obscene insult was required. Prostitutes, whatever their status during the rest of the year, were essential; bears, cocks and other symbols of lechery abounded in the iconography; massive representations of the penis, plain in Naples or disguised as enormous sausages in Königsberg, were carried in procession through the streets. Since the object of the performance was to expose what was concealed, it was natural that conduct to which shame attached should be a favourite target for exposure. But the display of sexuality was no more binding, at least in this early period of Carnival, than the display of more or less symbolically refined violence and hostility. The days of Carnival, as its best historian the Spaniard Julio Caro Baroja says, are days 'when the collective expression of envy, anger and enmity is legitimate'; a climate of fear and insecurity, of exposure to authorised violence rendered anonymous by the wearing of masks, must be maintained and accepted. In well-regulated cities at times of no particular stress, the obligations of aversion might be met by the trading of insults, the throwing of rotten eggs, or a bit of symbolic theft; but it was in the nature of the occasion that real violence, individual assassination or collective riot, was always likely to occur. Examples from Switzerland and Corsica make it plain that the 1580 carnival of Romans in Dauphiné, chronicled by Emmanuel Le Roy Ladurie in *The Peasants of Languedoc* (1966) and elsewhere, was following a reasonably well-trodden route. Here the symbolic hostility of three ritual fraternities, sharpened by a variety of exterior tensions at the time of the Wars of Religion, escalated into civil war and a small massacre; what seems more significant than the riot itself is that most of the population does not appear to have noticed that anything much had gone wrong. Somewhere between symbolic and genuine violence one must put the carnival games, which included early forms of football, then as now a satisfying outlet for collective hostility. The Spaniards developed a theologically elegant version of the game where the object was to deposit in the territory of the other side a ball into which the collected dirty linen of one's own had been ritually packed.

Arguments about whether the function of Carnival was to overturn or to maintain Society seem pointless, since there existed no such thing. If it took what we should call a political tone, putting the pope or the militant reformer Zwingli, Henri III or Cardinal Mazarin in the place of the figure to be burned, or harassing the officers of justice and taxation, this was because these were members of the body of Christ whose position gave them opportunities denied to others for infecting it with concupiscence and ill feeling. The world was turned upside-down to see what was crawling about underneath.

The real mystery about the feast is why it came into existence in some regions of Christendom rather than others: in, that is, Italy, including the islands, the Iberian peninsula, most of France, Switzerland and much of Germany, but less or not at all in north-west France, the British Isles, the Netherlands except for a southern fringe, north Germany or Scandinavia. One cannot put this distribution down to the Reformation, which it pre-dated, and must allow for the capacity of the feast to spread by imitation, since it was certainly taken up by the Jews, and apparently by the Russians as well. Carnival is of its nature something to do with penance, and I suggest that it is in the history of penance that we ought to look for an explanation of its origins and the limits of its diffusion. The regions of northern and north-western Europe which eat pancakes on Shrove Tuesday and do not celebrate Carnival were the regions where in the early Middle Ages the penitential tariff had been invented and received, and where confession and penance had always been individual matters; the liturgical procedure of public penance had been the tradition of the specifically Roman, and then of the Carolingian, West. Carnival, it would seem, had come into existence where a tradition of public confession and penance had been left in the air by the further progress of privacy after 1215.

(iii) Penance and Indulgence

While the remission of sins was in the textbooks the effect of a threefold action of contrition, confession and satisfaction performed in private between an individual sinner and an individual priest, it was in practice governed, like marriage, by an unwritten tradition that sin was a visible and social matter to be redeemed by acts as visible and social as the Passion of Christ. Not that there was any shortage of contrition, rather the reverse; but its spontaneous expression largely overflowed the sacramental channel provided to contain it. In the first place the tradition of public penance was visibly present in the operations of the Church courts, whose business was to deal with public sin and public reconciliation; and though their fees were unpopular and their activities tending to be restricted to matrimonial questions by the jealousy of competing jurisdictions, their operations continued to attract a wide degree of general support. This was notably true in matters of slander and defamation. The jurisdictions which superseded them were obliged to borrow their methods, since these were deeply ingrained in social practice.

But, whether theologians wished it or no, the tradition was almost equally present in the field of sacramental penance, which claimed to be dealing only with the interior man. Since 1215 people had been required to acknowledge their sins annually to the priest of the parish, or to some other legally qualified priest, and to carry out the satisfactory penance which would be enjoined on them, before they could be admitted to receive their Easter communion. The obligation was not very popular, but by the fifteenth century all but a few of them were fulfilling it. They were also, and a good deal more spontaneously, confessing their sins in the shadow of death. In either case, the sacrament represented a moment of critical transition: for the community and for the individual, a passage from a baptised but sinful condition into a supernatural state of 'grace', a passage from particularity towards membership of the whole body of Christ, a reconciliation to God and the neighbour. The characterisation may seem anachronistic. The penitential regime which, in the words of a speaker at the Council of Trent, 'reconciled all the members of Christ' to one another, restored the condition of supernatural peace to a Christian community whose wholeness had been vitiated by the sin of its members, and enabled them to pray together in charity for God's forgiveness of the sinner, was not the regime which formally prevailed at the close of the Middle Ages. Nor was it presupposed by the arguments of theologians fascinated by the power of binding and loosing which they held to reside in the hands of the priest. But the unilateral reconciliation to God of which they treated was not an adequate description of late medieval confession.

At death-bed confessions, for which we possess a vast body of documentation in the contents of wills, the crucial matter was the seeking and giving of pardon for offences committed against others or those committed by others against oneself. As it had been in the knightly death-scenes of the *Song of Roland,* so it continued to be. In Paris, as late as the middle of the seventeenth century, we are told by the French historian Pierre Chaunu with his wonted statistical precision, 57.5 per cent of wills required the heirs of the dying to make reparation for offences committed by the testator against others, and 42.4 per cent granted pardon for offences committed by others against him.[5] We can be pretty sure that in 1400 the percentage in each case would have been a good deal nearer 100. The habit of death-bed restitution for the offence of usury, often remarked on by economic historians, was a particular instance of a universal practice. Confession and restitution were for the dying an essential incident in the passage of the Christian towards an unsullied membership of the community of believers.

Both death-bed confession and the annual confession of Lent entailed for the penitent a duty of reconciliation with his neighbour. The main difference between them was that the average soul felt little enthusiasm for the task without the stimulus of an impending confrontation with his maker or the expectation of reciprocity which might accrue from the 'truce of death'. Apart from concubinage, the most frequent reason why people failed to fulfil the obligation of annual confession was that they were in a state of hostility with a neighbour, and proposed so to continue; and if, as seems usually the case, they were sufficiently afraid of exclusion from communion and community to come to confession, they came in no very different frame of mind. Except in the case of sexual sins, where shame seems to have been a governing instinct and it was often difficult or embarrassing for them to say anything at all, they came by all accounts in an aggressive and self-righteous mood, determined not to concede their own faults without emphasising the superior iniquity of others. They acted on the assumption, probably correct, that they had better do for their neighbour what it would be foolish to trust him to do for himself.

One may characterise their behaviour as a failure to rise to the standards demanded of them by theologians, but find a number of reasons for it. Some resisted the principle of self-accusation, in which the moral and psychological virtue of confession was held to lie, as a violation of the ethics of honour; others doubted the reliability of priests; many were certainly unable to recount their doings under the abstract categories which they were instructed to use, or to envisage actions as sinful except in a context of actual human relations. Their behaviour also expressed the positive conviction that sin was a state of offence inhering in communities rather than in individuals, and may have reflected the gospel injuction to 'tell the church' if their brothers had offended against them. The annual practice of the sacrament tended to encourage people in this view: even though, apparently with some exceptions in Germany, it was no longer formally speaking a collective rite, it was likely to be a more or less communal occasion, which normally occurred at the beginning of Holy Week. Writers and councils insisted that the priest was to receive his penitents not in a cell or sacristy but in some publicly visible part of the church, so that their communications were likely to be witnessed at no great distance by the assembled body of their neighbours. The ritual of absolution involved the laying of a hand by the priest on the head of a penitent, a public act by which the sinner was restored to the social communion of the Church, and seen to be so restored. The granting of absolution was contingent on the penitent's performing visible acts of reparation for his sin. In so far as the party offended was God, the acts were those of sacramental satisfaction, and these, according to the theologians, were what completed the sacrament; but where the party offended was also the neighbour, the reparatory act was that of restitution. According to theologians, restitution did not figure as a part of the sacramental sequence; yet without it, as without the laying aside of enmity, the process of reconciliation to God would not be achieved. All authors of advice to confessors spent a great deal of time in discussing restitution, obsessed as they might well be by the problem of reconciling it with privacy; the problem occurred also with strictly sacramental satisfactions which would naturally reveal to curious or prurient neighbours the nature of the sin in question. These problems are vividly conveyed by the quantity of advice offered to priests about what to do with a wife who confessed to an adulterous relationship from which a child had been born understood by her husband to be his own. The absolution of the woman for her sin was one thing, the calculation of its social consequences quite another. In the fulfilment of his responsibility for the exterior maintenance of the marriage alliance, not to mention the prevention of war between the families and a foreseeable chain of murders and further adulteries, the priest was nearly always advised to instruct the wife that she might not relieve her conscience by telling her husband what she had done. In his function as confessor he was called to be a counsellor and diplomat, dealing with the interests of the community at large and procuring the peace of the Church, as well as a guardian of the secret passage between the soul and God. This was not quite the world of Graham Greene.

Between the time of Gerson and that of Luther, the genuinely private conception of confession was certainly making progress. Thomas Tentler, drawing on the confessional manuals, has insisted on the interior disciplinary and consolatory function of the sacrament—what Luther called the medicining of sick consciences—and on its less attractive consequences like a growth of scrupulosity among penitents and the pedantic scrutiny of conjugal behaviour. One can ask how much of this penetrated the popular practice of confession, but it does seem likely that the diffusion of manuals, particularly after the invention of printing, reinforced the trend towards privacy. This was furthered by a multiplication of personal confessors among the nobility; and more generally by the failure of the parish clergy to maintain a monopoly of confession against the friars. It can be illustrated by two practical developments of the fifteenth century. One was a novel concern with the confession of children: there seems to have been a distinct shift downwards in the age from which the obligation to confess was thought to apply, from somewhere about 14 to somewhere about 7. Gerson seems to have been here a real pathfinder, and it must be obvious that if young children were to be considered suitable for the sacrament it could not have as a prime purpose the settlement of social conflicts. This concern went along with a rapid growth in the fifteenth century of the idea of confession as a medium of instruction, and with a proliferation of the little guides to confession, expounding the deadly sins and the Ten Commandments, the *Pater*, *Ave* and Apostles' Creed, which were the precursors of sixteenth-century catechisms. It was also from about 1400, Gerson here again being the principal initiator, that the notion of frequent confession, that is to say a monthly or otherwise regular event outside a ritual context, began to be proposed to the laity.

These were important developments for the future. For the time being, sacramental penance retained for the average penitent and the average priest characteristics which attached it to the penitential regimes of the past: its location among the rituals of Lent and the death-bed, and its connection with the performance of exterior acts of satisfaction.

Satisfaction was certainly not what it had been. The drastic penitential machinery of the earlier Middle Ages had been replaced by a modest regime of prayer and almsdeeds; the seventeenth-century English Catholic priest who imposed on his penitent a satisfaction of three *Paters*, three *Aves*, three Creeds, and the giving of 'three pence to three poor folks' was doing much what his predecessors would have done.[6] In the thirteenth century, there had been a conflict between those who held that without a penance proportionate to the sin forgiveness was uncertain, and those who wished to ensure universal confession by keeping sacramental penance to a minimum. There had also been a general worry that priests were imposing inadequate penances. But by the fifteenth, it seems to have been accepted that sacramental penance was largely symbolic. Under the influence of Aquinas, the notion made headway that penance was as much 'medicinal', or directed to reforming the future conduct of the sinner, as vindictive, or directed to restoring an objective social balance; the principal orthodox theologian of Luther's time, Cajetan, could affirm that the medicinal function was the only one that mattered. At the same time, and for the same reasons, the idea that a satisfactory penance was something which could appropriately be performed, for a consideration, by somebody other than the sinner was becoming difficult for theologians to understand. Yet it would not be true to say that by the Reformation all satisfaction was symbolic, or that the average person would have wished it to be so. For him, as for the theologians, *culpa* or guilt was one thing and *poena* or penalty another. As Luther observed in the Ninety-Five Theses of 1517, good Christians still believed firmly in the need to undergo painful penances if their sins were to be forgiven. Hence the depth of popular feeling about Lent, a collective rite by which public penitence had been not so much superseded as consolidated; placed between Carnival and Easter, it was so closely related to confession as to make up a good deal of what was lacking in the satisfactory aspect of the sacrament.

For any healthy and normally occupied adult, Lent was indeed forty days in the wilderness, broken only by an interval in the middle whose popularity indicates the dismal character of the season it alleviated. Veiled from his sight in funereal purple, the friendly figures of Christ, of Mary and the saints were covered and could not be reached for help or consolation; preachers summoned him relentlessly to the distasteful task of contemplating himself. Behind the banner of a gaunt old woman advancing with an exiguous fish on an otherwise bare platter, he went forward to the conquest of his flesh. Admittedly, in the passage from personal ordeal to collective exercise, the penitential machinery had lost some of its teeth. The Christian was no longer forbidden to bear arms, and the machinery of legal dispute did not cease to grind. Married couples were no longer obliged to abstain from intercourse for the whole forty days. Yet considerable vestiges of what had been a rigorous prohibition still remained. There was a ban on intercourse for some days before Easter communion; total Lenten abstinence, though not required by theologians, was still encouraged as an act of devotion, and the original prohibition seems to have been maintained in some dioceses; the parish clergy were not necessarily *au fait* with what the theologians said. Seasonal statistics of conception, when they become available around 1600, suggest that sexual abstinence was quite common. Marriage and the associated festivities of kinship were prohibited, and most of the brothels were closed.

The fast itself seems by a long way the most deeply ingrained of all the observances of the period. It consisted of an absolute ban, from Ash Wednesday to Holy Saturday including Sundays, on the eating of meat, to which no qualification was made before the Reformation; and a further ban on what were called white-meats or *lacticinia*, a term which covered any food derived from animals or poultry like milk, butter, cheese and eggs. The Easter egg presumably originated in the days of the larger ban, which seems to have been generally respected until about 1400. Thereafter it was easier to get a dispensation for *lacticinia*, or *Butterbrief*; by the end of the century these were being bought on a scale sufficient to pay for the *Tour de Beurre* of Rouen cathedral and greatly to irritate Luther. The diffusion of the *Butterbrief* may possibly reveal a change in northern cooking habits, and it is not clear that it meant a general decline in lay asceticism. In England north of the Trent white-meats were still taboo at the time of the Reformation, though the south had apparently become more lax. For most people Lent still meant what it had meant to the Catholics of Montaillou around 1300: a diet of vegetables, and of fish if they could afford it, which with the development of the northern fishing industry in the fifteenth century it seems likely that they could. This slimming diet was to be consumed at a single meal, in principle not before nightfall, though popular and monastic hunger had been drawing it inexorably forward towards noon; this seems to have been general practice in the fifteenth century, along with a little something in the evening. Even with these moderations it was quite a rigorous regime, and it obtained, outside Lent, on Fridays, and sometimes Saturdays, three Ember Days every quarter, and the eve of a number of feasts which varied according to their local importance.

This was a domestic observance, one of the few domestic rites which medieval Catholicism possessed. It was naturally more impressive in households whose material circumstances were comparatively easy. But it also meant a great deal to humble people: to the Portuguese driven to eat meat because there was a famine of Lenten victuals, who brought their case to the bishop in considerable disarray; to the woman in Montaillou, fetching her turnips back from the field for an ascetic *déjeuner*, who fell out with a well-fed heretic on the road; to the poor of Flanders who were allowed milk and eggs at the close of the fifteenth century because fish and vegetables were too dear. Lent meant something to every Catholic householder and his family: sickness and age were not yet regarded as qualifications for relief. Very hard physical work was so regarded, though it is not clear that this made much difference in practice. The only real exceptions were beggars and vagabonds who had no reliable means of support and no fixed abode. The compromises of the lax were balanced by the austerities of those who fasted more than they were obliged to do. From the fifteenth century to the seventeenth, in England, France and the Netherlands, they abstained from alcoholic drink (which had long since ceased to be an obligation), ate nothing but bread and water for the whole of Lent, added fasting Wednesdays to fasting Fridays, waited until nightfall to break their fast. In Flanders it was held that a voluntary fast on bread and water of twelve consecutive Fridays was an assured means of salvation.

In the long run (if Luther was the long run) the ever more intense concentration of mind and feelings on the reality of the satisfactory sufferings of Christ would probably reduce the pressure on the devout to pacify God by a superabundance of penitential acts. In the short run, it had the opposite effect. The traditional 'common penance' of pilgrimage, though not quite what it had been in the time of the Crusades, was still a more daunting event than might be gathered from Chaucer's civilised example. It was the one physical penance which might still be imposed by a priest in confession, and in regions of more rigorous practice like the north of England Catholics could still be found in 1700 at holy wells and springs, kneeling up to their necks in icy water to say their penitential prayers, probably for fornication. The hazards of the long-range pilgrimages to St James at Compostela and Our Lady at Rocamadour, from seasickness upwards, were such as to make them a satisfaction acceptable to the victims of violence or their friends; in northern France and the Netherlands an agreement on the offender's part to make such a pilgrimage was a standard feature in the arbitration of disputes. It is hard to know whether these judicial pilgrims were more numerous than those who went spontaneously to fulfil their vows, redeem their sins, see the Holy Places, visit their name-saints, claim indulgences, or have a change of air. Whatever their motives, they passed on setting out into the same official condition of liminality or weightlessness which marked, like baptismal exorcism or Lent, the passage from past profanity towards future holiness. I see no reason to suppose that a practice which has thrived during the nineteenth and twentieth centuries was on its last legs in the fifteenth. It was not very popular with the authorities, secular or spiritual, who had their reasons for wishing people to stay at home; during the century from Gerson to Erasmus it suffered from a rise of domestic piety and the increasing impatience with symbolic behaviour of the learned. In popular devotion it had to compete with the urge towards a more realistic and dramatic identification with the sufferings of Christ, which in Italy from the middle of the fourteenth century had taken the form of collective flagellation.

Launched as a more satisfying version of pilgrimage in an atmosphere much like that of the early Crusades, the flagellant movement fulfilled in a collective way the principal function of judicial pilgrimage: it attempted, by representing the patience of Christ in the hands of his enemies, to effect the subjugation of the passions of hostility and to procure peace and reconciliation among Christians. For some flagellants the practice of their discipline became a vehicle for the satisfaction of sin manifestly superior to sacramental penance, and the papacy condemned them for the opinion at the close of the fourteenth century. But their drift was superorthodoxy rather than heresy, scarcely differing except by its publicity from the hair-shirts of such as Thomas More. They certainly failed to dislodge conventional pilgrimage, and their fashion had passed, at least in Italy, by the mid-fifteenth century; thereafter their institutions, the orthodox fraternities of *disciplinati* and the like, successfully developed a less heroic mode of devotion which combined symbolic discipline with actual charity.

Flagellation might rise and fall: it seems to have risen in Spain as it was declining in Italy; but the conviction that visible satisfaction was essential for the pacification of God and one's neighbour had not weakened by the sixteenth century. The miller Menocchio, who thought that the only purpose of going to confession was to discover the appropriate satisfaction for one's sin, and that there was no need for it if you could find this out otherwise, spoke for a level of instinct too deep to be reached by Erasmus's elegant proof that this was not what the gospels meant. This is the first thing to be borne in mind when thinking about the penitential issue most in evidence on the eve of the Reformation: the issue of indulgences. For questions about indulgence were questions about satisfaction. The institution had its origins in the earlier regime of public penance, and the term applied to the remission, diminution or conversion of the penal satisfaction imposed on the sinner in the course of his readmission to the community of the Church. It also covered the undertaking by the Church to offer its prayers or *suffragia* to God that he would likewise be reconciled. It represented charity in the courts of penitential justice, and continued to represent it after the system of public penance had decayed.

By 1400 various other things had happened to indulgence. It had become attached to a variety of works, of which the most important was the crusade, but including public improvements like bridge- or church-building; it had become established that these works could be performed by proxy, or commuted for money; the granting of it had become in effect a papal monopoly; and in answer to the objection that sins could not be forgiven for which satisfaction had not been made, theologians like Aquinas had come up with the notion of the treasure of the Church. The idea in itself was a reasonable deduction from a feature of the early medieval penitential system which Anselm had evoked in his doctrine of the Redemption. Satisfactory penance due from one person could be made by another, provided the relation between the two parties was sufficiently intimate that what was done by one of them could be taken, by God and by the Church, as being done by the other. The idea of transferable merit was not stretched by the assumption that the sufferings of Christ were sufficient to make up for any possible amount of satisfaction which the sins of Christians might require; and not stretched very much by the argument that the saints in heaven and the meritorious faithful on earth could assist the sinner by passing over to him the merit they had acquired by satisfaction in excess of their own needs. The second point was disputed, for the doctrine of vicarious satisfaction seemed to imply that the transfer of merit could only be effective where there was a particular relation of charity or kinship; but nobody could really argue with the first. From the popes' point of view the doctrine of the treasury of the Church, once discovered, meant that no limit could be assigned to their power to remit satisfactory penalties.

Indulgence was therefore not a substitute for sacramental

penance: it assumed that the sinner was repentant and had confessed his sins, and simply enabled him to forgo the penitential act imposed. In its earlier phases it was a positive incentive for people to confess their sins; by the fifteenth century the rule was that the obligation could be met by normal annual confession in the year preceding the granting of indulgence, which helped to meet the widespread anxiety about dying without the opportunity to confess. Nor, though it upset theologians, was there really much of a problem in the wording of later indulgences, which added the remission of *culpa* or guilt to that of *poena* or satisfaction: in thinking about indulgences people were thinking about *poena*, and the general view was that if you looked after the *poena* the *culpa* would look after itself. The real difficulty was created by the decline of the satisfactory element in sacramental penance, which appeared to take away the motive for seeking indulgence, but in fact supplied a different and perhaps stronger one. Since it implied that reckoning for sin would be postponed from this life to the next, it naturally created a demand for indulgence in respect of the pains of purgatory. The popes from 1300 onwards seem to have had no doubt that their power as custodians of the treasure of the Church extended to purgatory; it was therefore their duty as well as their pleasure to add indulgence to the existing modes of prayer and sacrifice by which the living performed their obligations to the souls of the dead. The unofficial provision of such indulgences, practised in particular by the Franciscans of Assisi, was finally regularised when the Franciscan Pope Sixtus IV in 1476 granted a model indulgence, for anyone contributing to the rebuilding of the church at Saintes in western France, of absolute remission from the pains of purgatory to kindred and friends suffering there. The model served for the multitude of similar indulgences granted during the next half-century. It is hard to blame preachers of indulgences for telling their hearers that when their money dropped in the box a soul of their choice would fly up to heaven. This arresting image was not invented by Johan Tetzel during his fateful tour of Germany in 1517, but was a commonplace which had already been condemned by the Sorbonne in 1482; the indulgence he was selling, ostensibly for the rebuilding of St Peter's in Rome, was in fact rather cautiously phrased, though not much notice was taken of this in preaching it. Its author, Pope Leo X, had already brought theory into line with practice by stating that in respect of their qualification for indulgences there was no difference at all between the living and the dead.

There were several reasons for objecting to this development. Bishops and clergy objected because it seemed likely to undercut masses for the dead and deprive them of much of their income; theologians because they wanted to maintain some kind of connection with the historic *suffragia*, and had never been quite convinced that the pope had jurisdiction over the souls in purgatory. They raised the rhetorical question why, since the pope could liberate souls from purgatory, he did not liberate them all at once. Luther's Ninety-Five Theses were a compendium of such complaints, and though it is anachronistic to think of them as the start of the Reformation, they did touch something more fundamental about the disarray of Catholicism than it has recently been usual to believe. One can sympathise with the Renaissance popes for finding the simultaneous claims of humanity and profit too strong to resist, and for doing their bit, as they saw it, to further the salvation of souls. I doubt if one can acquit them of Luther's charge of irresponsibly playing about with the penitential instinct. It did not cement the solidarity of the Church when the civilised Leo X, who thought satisfaction for sin a barbarous anachronism, scattered remission for punishments in which he did not believe in front of a population persuaded that sin would always have to be paid for in one way or another.

4 The Social Miracle

(i) Fraternity

In the *Vita Nuova*, written at the beginning of the fourteenth century, Dante described his feelings when the young Beatrice greeted him in a Florentine street. In part these were the individual emotions of Pre-Raphaelite romantic love. But what a genuinely pre-Raphaelite vision would have picked up was that they were also social emotions. The greeting was a formal social act implying relationship, the effect was a *coup de foudre* not simply about the girl but about the social universe as a whole, a love which instantaneously occupied the entire social field and burned away the passions of hostility felt towards any person within it. In the Italian city of Dante's time, this was a feeling worth recording: it was a miracle, and Dante so described it. I take this vision of social beatitude to be conveying a number of convictions held as axiomatic by orthodox Catholics from Dante's time to Luther's, and will risk expounding them as follows. The state of charity, meaning social integration, was the principal end of the Christian life, and any people that claimed to be Christian must embody it somehow, at some time, in this world. It was against nature to expect that general charity could prevail as a rule of everyday life, since by the course of nature friendship with some entailed enmity to others: hence partial, segmental or occasional communion was better than none at all, half a eucharistic loaf better than no bread. When perfect communion did happen it was to be regarded as an extraordinary deliverance, an intervention in the facts of nature bringing who knew what other deliverances in its wake. Finally, the presence of charity in the world depended to a considerable degree upon the diligent maintenance of a certain number of outward formalities of which the act of salutation, though perhaps the simplest, was perhaps also the most important. In the pursuit of the whole, salutation was the beginning, salvation the end.

The institution which most spontaneously embodied this frame of mind was the fraternity. Fraternities, the most characteristic expressions of late medieval Christianity, have been regarded as substitute kindreds for those who did not possess natural ones, but they were clearly something more than this. At the least, as John Hale says, they satisfied 'an appetite for association beyond [economic] needs and beyond the circle of the kin';[7] at the best, they embodied sacred Christian kinship as opposed to profane consanguinity. They did so, in principle, more purely than godparenthood, since they represented confraternity without compaternity, indeed without paternity in any sense, including that of lordship; to people for whom brotherhood with Christ was a more compelling guarantee of Christian hope than sonship of the Father they offered Christian solidarity as an object of free choice. To millions of Latin Christians, between the thirteenth century and the sixteenth, they presented the opportunity of conforming themselves to Christ more exactly than the next man, while drawing upon instincts which were universal.

Institutional fraternity was not an invention of the century or two preceding the Reformation, nor a response to the Black Death or to the political or economic difficulties of the age; the plague may well have given it a new lease of life, as did almost any dramatic or disturbing event in the history of Christendom. It can be found at any period after the conversion of the West and seems to have become universal from the later thirteenth century. Its diffusion owed a lot to the friars, who were institutional brothers themselves. As an ideal it does not seem to have been notably restricted by barriers of status or occupation, though individual fraternities certainly were so restricted. Except in the case of the very poor, who could not have afforded the modest entrance fee, and probably with some qualification made for the nobility, they flourished throughout the population, in the country as in towns, among women as among men. Although there are signs of a drift towards oligarchy inside fraternities during the fifteenth century, the principle was, to quote a Breton example, 'that we are all brothers in God and that there is no precedence before him'; in some cases the incorporation of persons of differing status was a formal object of the fraternal institution. Allowing that many people were members of more than one, it seems inconceivable to put the number of fraternity members at less than a tenth of the adult population, and a proportion twice as large as this would seem extremely probable; they quite often recruited the majority of a local community, sometimes the whole of it. Except for remote parts which possessed kinship institutions of exceptional strength, like Gaelic Ireland, there seem to have been no geographical limits to their diffusion.

Like the trade gilds, which were only a particular species of the genus, fraternities were great inventors of ritual. The ritual of entry into brotherhood or sisterhood involved an oath, or more appropriately a kiss: in a London gild 'every brother and sister, in tokening of love and charity and peace, at receiving shall kiss other of them that ben there'. Charity, 'fraternal dilection' according to Christ's commandment, was accepted as an obligation. The rituals of participation were greeting, meeting and eating. Salutation in the course of everyday life, as Dante witnesses, was no light matter: as an obligation it appears in the earliest Anglo-Saxon gilds, and was as universal for fraternity members as for penitents hoping for absolution after confession. The purpose of meeting, normally four times a year including one main annual meeting, was not simply to elect officers, admit new members and demonstrate 'worship' or status, but 'to intercommune'; there were fines for absence, and strict regulations against noisy, lewd or offensive words or behaviour. The fraternity feast usually followed the annual meeting, and represented the central act of fraternity. In earlier days the terms *convivium* (festive meal) and gild had been practically interchangeable in northern Europe, and *charité*, used to describe fraternities in Normandy, still meant the *prandium caritatis* or love-feast. As such it continued to take up a great deal of space in fraternity statutes, and even more in the comments of critics and the legislation of ecclesiastical authorities, who from the earliest times treated it as an occasion for gluttony and disorder; especially from the sixteenth century, they dismissed it as a waste of money which could be put to better charitable use. Drinking, and compulsory dancing, were alternatives or additions to the meal.

The characteristic of Christian relationship was peace, the peace which equalled friendship, the peace in the feud, not peace the opposite of war or the effect of victory. Brotherhood and peace-keeping were associated throughout the Middle Ages, sometimes, as in the case of the Holy Brotherhood of fifteenth-century Castile, simply in the form of a police force, but more intimately by the creation of bonds of Christian kinship among those who would otherwise be at enmity or feud. The theme was universal, but particularly strong in the fraternities of northern Italy. Fraternities were created in an attempt to transcend the conflicts of papalist Guelfs and imperialist Ghibellines, or family faction in general. The peacemaking motive, rather than individual hysteria inspired by plague or other visitations, lay behind the popularity of the flagellant brotherhoods launched at moments of great popular emotion. At the launching in 1399 of a sort of Campaign for Nuclear Disarmament called the *Bianchi*, or *Whites*, towns and individuals competed in peacemaking rituals, 'and everyone thought himself happy if he could get in first in giving the kiss of peace to him by whom he had been offended'.[8] Such moments of general reconciliation were the principal objective of popular preaching in Italy and elsewhere; the adoption of the flagellant discipline by penitential fraternities implied, not a surrender to the delights of masochism, but a desperate recognition of the primacy of hatred among the natural passions. Historians have not usually thought these emotional occasions of much lasting effect, and they may well be right: one would hardly claim that the institution of peacemaking fraternities by a bishop in sixteenth-century Corsica had eradicated feud from the island. Still, invoking the social miracle was probably as efficient as other methods of pacification which might have been tried, and it was certainly more attractive. In less dramatic circumstances the obligation of peace required members to abstain from going to law with each other and to settle disputes by arbitration. Complicated procedures were frequently laid down; statutes can be found requiring that if one party were to appeal from them to the law, the warden and arbitrators were to testify in court on behalf of the other. The activity was clearly a real attempt to fulfil the Augustinian principle that lawsuits were a form of enmity which Christians should avoid; it was surely influential in creating the general consensus in early modern Europe that disputes between neighbours should be settled by arbitration, not taken to court.

All these were expressions of charity as people understood it: and charity in our own more conventional sense played a large and perhaps increasing part in fraternal activity, though before the sixteenth century it was normally confined to members. Brothers who fell into poverty and impotence were to be assisted with money from funds which, like those accumulated by the *Scuole Grandi*, the stem-fraternities of Venice, could be quite large. Some gilds made interest-free loans to members. Free lending of food or goods, stock or hospitality, was probably more important in the countryside. Usury, according to the biblical command about not lending upon usury to one's brother, was a disqualification for membership and a ground for expulsion. Towards outsiders the prohibition was perhaps loosened from the beginning of the sixteenth century when the public pawnshops known as *monti di pietà*, and their practice of making small loans to the poor at 5 per cent, were declared by the pope to be legitimate. So far as I know, lending at interest was never held to be legitimate among members. In short the fraternities seem to have made a fair stab at the idea of free Christian lending propounded by Luther until experience taught him caution. It is also worth insisting, since they are often assumed to have been confined to inhabitants of towns, that agricultural co-operation loomed quite as large as welfare and loans in fraternity statutes, and that in some regions, like southern France, they had a great deal to do with the construction of rural community. This was especially true of smaller villages and inaccessible parts.

Charity also, and more as time went on, meant a concern for the welfare of the dead, and for the proper conduct of the rites of dying. Conflict between fraternities and families was fairly common, especially over wills and inheritances, and we cannot therefore regard fraternities as simply making up for a lack of family support. But the natural area of their activity for souls seems to have ranged between the aristocracy, who after 1400 would provide for themselves and their friends through chantries and otherwise, and the poor who would depend on the parish or, for burial, on service fraternities specially created for the purpose. In the north fraternities hired chaplains to say mass for the souls of dead members; in Italy they were normally more active, meeting their obligations towards the dead by prayers said in common. By the fifteenth century some of the smarter English gilds were admitting dead persons to brotherhood, an apparently illogical concession which probably meant that the merits of the fraternity could be employed for the benefit of a member's relation, so long as he paid an entry fee on his behalf. As in employing chaplains, they were somewhat stretching the scriptural injunction to pray for one another that they might be saved.

Despite some signs of decay, like plural membership, the fraternity on the eve of the Reformation seems in general to have taken seriously the obligation of Christian brotherhood among its members. Its relation with the world outside was a more complicated matter, since brotherhood, to borrow Benjamin Nelson's phrase, entailed otherhood, the differentiation of inside and outside moralities described by Max Weber. Brothers were sworn to secrecy, to give information of danger impending to the brotherhood, to stick up for a brother or for the fraternity as a whole if reflections were passed on him or it by outsiders, to support one another at law. Except where they were sharpened by heresy or, as in Dalmatia, by racial antagonism between Latins and Slavs, their conflicts were mainly symbolic; such were the disputes among craft gilds about precedence on public occasions which fill the chronicles of late medieval towns. But well before their credit was undermined by humanist ethics and Reformation theology, they had been unpopular with authorities, who often found them a pest and from time to time made efforts to abolish them. The magistrates of Florence were probably right to complain that they caused stirs and discord in the city, though this was partly their own fault for failing to make public use of them, as the Venetians were to do.

Perhaps in response to such criticism, fraternities in the fifteenth century made efforts towards extending their practice of charity to the public at large. In the north Corpus Christi gilds looked after the celebration of the feast, including the mystery plays; the *misericordie* of Italy provided for the poor and founded hospitals; fraternities buried the dead and possibly taught Christian doctrine. Their activities were to grow into the 'new philanthropy' of the sixteenth century. But in general they continued to practise charity as a relationship between members, and their sectarian situation in the theoretically hierarchical and universal structure of the Church remained insecure. Unlike the relation between friars and parish clergy, which it resembled and to which it was connected by the fraternal propaganda of the friars, the relation between fraternities and parishes in the late medieval Church does not seem to have attracted historians. Yet it is rather crucial to a judgement of what the institution was actually like. I venture the following remarks. We should not regard the parish as necessarily a pre-existing datum into which fraternities were going to have to fit themselves some-how. Parochial formation and fraternity expansion were roughly contemporary processes, and though the parish network was substantially complete by 1400, there were plenty of gaps left at the Reformation. It was weak in the mountains, and in areas without much village settlement like Ireland. Otherwise it proceeded more rapidly on the virgin soil of the north than in Mediterranean Europe, where older forms of ecclesiastical structure persisted. Hence fraternal institutions might often find no parish structure to compete with, and a brotherhood might form the original community of worship, until such time as its chapel might be erected into a parish church. Extreme cases of this sequence exist in Dalmatia, where the fraternal might precede the parochial organisation by two to three hundred years. Something like it seems to have been not uncommon in the rural north, particularly the subalpine north, of Italy, and also in Provence and the Massif Central, where the Pentecost feasts of the *confréries du Saint-Esprit* provided the annual occasion of universal sociability. In such cases fraternity and parish were hardly at odds; nor were they so in Italian cities, where the parish was a feeble plant. In northern Europe there was more of a struggle: Nicholas of Cusa, attempting to reform Germany in the 1450s, prohibited the erection of new fraternities as detracting from the honour and rights of parish churches. Here, as in England, there was in most regions a parochial structure in place. Where a large single fraternity grew within the boundaries of a parish it was likely to promote the kind of lay intervention in public worship which became more visible in England after the Reformation: brotherhoods encouraged attendance at mass, augmented stipends, provided for extra mas-ses, rebuilt churches which had fallen down as a result of war or plague. Where small fraternities proliferated within or across the parish boundary, there would follow a multiplication of fraternity chapels in the parish church, and disputes between officers of gilds and curates or parish officials: the kind of jostling which gave depth to the representations of ritual unity so prominent in the closing Middle Ages. Faced by the twenty-one fraternities of Wittenberg, Luther objected that they were a misguided way of trying to achieve a state of Christian love of which the proper agent was the Eucharist. It seems an ungenerous thought, for he was in various ways an heir to their achievements.

(ii) Community

Some time in the middle of the sixteenth century, a small community living in a remote branch of the Valtellina in the southern Alps decided to support a resident priest. They found one, agreed his salary and laid down the conditions of life he was to observe and the duties he was to perform. The conditions were that he was not to take a mistress, or if he must, find one elsewhere, not to gamble his income away, and in general to lead a decent and sober life. His functions were to say mass according to the wishes of the population, and to make peace among those who were at enmity.[9] In so far as the community did not constitute a parish, the priest's position was unusual: he had no tithes, and was apparently not required to administer other sacraments or to visit the sick and dying. Some might have wanted him to preach, or teach catechism. Otherwise his duties and the way of life thought appropriate to them were what would have been expected of any rural incumbent by a traditionally minded population from Chaucer's day to his. Chaucer's evangelical parson and his 'brother', the charitable ploughman, were images of the ideal. But the spontaneous attitude of the population of Forcola sopra Morbegna may suggest that they were not unreal, in an era when hostility to the clergy has been held to be a predominant popular feeling, and disputes between priests and parishes were certainly common. But then disputes between everybody were common, and priests who were more or less on a level with their flocks were more likely to get involved in them than the graduate or seminary-trained clergy of a later age. Hostility between priests and members of their flock was both a fact of life and a cliché of the books, and most of our knowledge of the pre-Reformation clergy, derived from the complaints of parishioners at episcopal visitations, is a result of it. It is hard to know whether the incidence of bad feeling between clergy and parishes was greater than that between people in general, but the relationship entailed a complex of elements—financial, sexual, ritual, legal, social and psychological—which formed a peculiarly combustible mixture.

The complaints, apart from the priest's failure to fulfil his ritual duties, or visit the sick and dying, turned on avarice, lechery and lack of charity. Complaints about avarice normally arose out of the tithe, or where this did not belong to the parson, out of things like burial fees. They seem the most common cause of irritation, though it would be excessive to take as normal G. R. Elton's memorable case of tithe and trouble at Hayes in Middlesex, where writs were flourished in church, vestments impounded, and the saying of mass (except on All Souls' Day) embargoed. It is also worth remembering that at the same time a great deal of money was being given voluntarily to the parish clergy, usually in return for extra parochial masses, and perhaps it is more of a wonder that most parishes did not complain than that many did. The problem with tithe and similar issues was that they were very likely to provoke lawsuits between the parson and some or all of the parish, which would be understood as a declaration of hostility and in extreme cases bring the parish as an embodiment of Christian society to a complete halt. Counter-charges of uncharitable or violent behaviour by the priest could be expected.

Such hostilities, as Gerson remarked, were likely to include a charge against the priest's chastity. For this reason historians have recently been inclined to dismiss as malicious gossip a high proportion of the charges of sexual incontinence brought against the pre-Reformation parish clergy, and in general they are probably right. Taking the long view, it would seem that after the institution of clerical celibacy by the eleventh-century Gregorian reform, what happened was a slow accommodation of the clergy to a difficult discipline, rather than the progressive collapse of an unnatural restriction, regularised at the Reformation. Efforts at quantification which have been made for dioceses in England and the rest of Europe suggest a clergy by 1500 continent in practice to a degree of 80 or 90 per cent. There were, however, considerable regional differences, in which the attitude of parishioners was probably fundamental. There seem to have been, particularly in the north-west, large areas where popular opinion, despite repeated official disclaimers, regarded any unchastity as a pollutant, a breach of contract and a threat to the efficacy of a priest's ritual functions. Here incontinency was an underground affair and clerical marriage, when it came, a cause of disgust and ridicule. This seems to have been the case in the north of England, and probably in much of France as well. Elsewhere, for just the reasons which counselled towns in southern France to maintain public brothels, people tended to make a distinction between monogamous concubinage (even if it produced children to serve on the altar) and irregular fornication, especially with the wives and daughters of the parish.

If the latter, as the greater evil and an infallible destroyer of parochial peace and charity, was to be avoided, the former had better be tolerated, and indeed organised. Allegations that formal arrangements to this effect were made at the reception of a priest into the community come from south Germany and Spain, and they seem to have been fairly widespread in alpine lands. Authorities like Gerson were prepared, however reluctantly, to see the point. Both rigour and connivance were probably extreme cases. We are perhaps nearer the norm with the case of a curate in the diocese of Lincoln, accused by the churchwardens of trying to rape a parishioner's wife and threatening her with a suit for adultery when she resisted, to whom two girls of the parish brought a 'babe of clouts' and asked him to christen it. The judge told the curate to keep away from women, and the parish to live together in charity.[10]

Since parishes were rarely backward in coming forward with charges against their priests, it seems reasonable to assume that in the majority of cases, where they kept silent, the priest was doing his job with fair conscientiousness, sensitivity and common sense. This was quite a feat, since as the hub of Christian society he had functions to perform which might seem inherently contradictory. He had (at least in the north, since notaries might do more or less the same job elsewhere) to serve the separate families at their baptisms, marriages and death-beds; keep his finger on their kin-relationships, their dowries, wills and burials; say mass for their living and their dead; defend their persons, offspring, beasts and possessions from malicious or diabolical interference. He had at the same time, for the sake of the parish as a whole, to criticise their misdeeds and avoid espousing their quarrels; whether at confession or more informally throughout the year, it was his business to procure reconciliation of their enmities through arbitration, satisfaction and rituals of togetherness performed in church, at the alehouse, or elsewhere. This was not something which got mentioned at visitations, since good news was no news; but it was a duty impressed on him from above and below, and was certainly as much practised before the Reformation as after. He had, finally, in face of a good deal of pressure for privacy, to maintain the church and churchyard as a place of public holiness where the parish could assemble together to combine sociability with the worship of God.

This was pre-eminently the function of the parish mass, sung at the high altar on Sundays and feast-days, and often by endowment on one or more weekdays as well. In law and practice a public occasion, it stood out from the private masses which multiplied in side-chapels, on weekdays, and outside parish churches. Despite the complaints of liturgists and reformers, it was not a contradiction that mass should be offered by the priest alone, in a ritual language, largely in silence and partly out of sight, and yet embody or create the sense of collective identity. In that respect it represented Durkheim's identification of the sacred with the collective. It represented something else where, as B. L. Manning put it, it possessed the 'human interest' of engaging with the socially particular as well as with the general; it performed the dramatic coup of eliciting the supernatural out of the mundane.

We need not suppose that congregations were ignorant of what the priest was doing on the altar, if only because his performance was frequently criticised. The average parishioner, who would probably not be up to that, nevertheless knew what he needed to know. He knew that the priest was making sacrifice and satisfaction for the living and for the dead; he knew that he would make God actually present in the Host before consuming it. If he was not a heretic or unbeliever he knew that this extraordinary event represented the best thing that could have happened in the universe, a deliverance from the powers of evil, a reconciliation of God and man from which any amount of consequential good might follow, in this world and the next. If he could say his paternoster, and had been to confession and communion, he knew that these effects were something to do with the painful tasks of repenting your sins and loving your neighbour. Nor do we have to suppose that he was not, in ways important to him, a participant, though more in some parts of the mass than in others.

The first part went to the end of the offertory, when the bread and wine were presented on the altar: one should imagine a good deal of noise, people coming late, walking or shuffling about, some talking, the occasional argument. There were some devout congregations who answered the priest at the beginning of this part of the mass, at the confession of sin *Confiteor*, or at the offertory prayer *Suscipiat*, where it ended. Usually their attention would be held if there was an offering to be made, as on feast- and communion-days; it would sharpen when the priest turned from the altar to make his announcements, read banns of marriage (sometimes to general laughter), and state the particular request being prayed for in his mass, or others commended to him. At this point of intense attention would occur what the English called the bedes and the French the *prône*: vernacular prayers for the spiritual and temporal authorities, the fruits of the earth, the sorts and conditions of men, friends, allies, relations, enemies; prayers for the living and the dead. The dead were certainly taking an increasing part of such prayers, but that did not necessarily lessen the concern with which the living would present their chorus of contradictory desires. To pray for themselves and all their own, as they were invited to do, for their security and welfare in this life and salvation in the next, was to pray against those, human and superhuman, who might threaten these; it was known that if you could get into the priest's commemoration of the dead the name of someone still alive, the power of the mass could kill him. If that was a thought people would probably suppress except in a crisis, as during the vendetta of French Catholics against King Henri III, there remained the extremely credible spectacle described by Langland of Envy cursing his neighbours during the bidding of the bedes, as the Wife of Bath lost her temper when somebody beat her to the altar steps at the offertory.

In short, until this point in the mass the parish was being itself: participating certainly, since it was doing no more than uniting the living and the dead with the act of sacrifice as the text of the mass required; but except for the unusually devout, who might be praying in corners, hardly undergoing an experience of the holy. The transformation might begin with a sermon, which would usually occur at this point if there was one. But normally it came when the bell rang and the *Sanctus* launched the priest and congregation into the silence of the canon or, as the Germans called it, *Stillmesse*. People knelt. The Church did not encourage them to know exactly what the priest was saying, on the grounds that if they did they would use such powerful words for conjuring and malice. But as his arms moved they knew he was preparing to make God present, as they would verify when the bell rang again and having bowed their heads they would lift them up and see him, round and white in the priest's fingers. For the devout as for the average soul, the elevation of the Host at the end of the Middle Ages was a moment of transcendental experience. After it the less than average, including the thirstier men, retired to the inn; the pious communed with their Saviour; the majority waited for the elevation to be repeated. Even if they had not forgotten their private existences, desires and terrors in the presence of the Host (advice on this subject would differ), they were probably somewhat nearer to that state of communion in which hostility became impersonal and retired beyond the borders of the community, to lurk in a dark exterior cast into more frightful shadow by the visible brightness of heaven among them. This at least was the message of one of the most popular and most long-lived of devotional inventions, the hymn *O Salutaris Hostia* first sung by fifteenth-century German congregations to the elevated Host:

> *O salutaris hostia,*
> *Quae coeli pandis ostium,*
> *Bella premunt hostilia,*
> *Da robur, fer auxilium.*

> (Victim and Deliverer
> Who openest the gates of Heaven,
> Our enemies are beating us down.
> Give strength to us, bring help.)

Without probably being able to explain, which is not necessarily to say without knowing, the difference between sacrifice and sacrament, they would feel, as the priest continued with the canon, that they were entering a further stage of the proceedings. They would be standing again, there would be a little more movement; what the priest was doing would become a little less mysterious. They would hear *Pater Noster*, and might join, silently or aloud, in its requests for daily bread, for deliverance from evil, and for the conditional forgiveness of their sins. They knew the condition and, fortified or chastened by the presence of the Host, reminded by the priest's *Pax Domini* or, if they were rich or lucky, by the new harmonies of the choir's *Dona nobis pacem*, they would prepare to accept from the altar the bond of peace and charity with their neighbours. This would be too much for some, who would either have left after the elevation or have refused to come at all. Those who remained would in some cases exchange the ancient kiss of peace, the *magnum sacramentum* of St Paul and St Augustine, men to men and women to women according to the rules, though not according to much-repeated stories. More often they would in turn kiss the pax, a painted image of Christ, or cross, or similar holy object brought round among them by the parish clerk, and try not to quarrel about who was to kiss it first. Invented by the English in the thirteenth century, the pax had been welcomed by the clergy, diffused through Christendom by the Franciscans, and was probably now accepted by most people as the holier, and possibly somewhat less binding, alternative. By the time the *Pax* was over the priest would be telling them that the mass was ended, and giving them his final blessing before they went out. The noise level would by now have returned to what it had been at the beginning.

It was a complaint of reformers, and was to be one of liturgists, that these masses deprived the population of the authentic vehicle of Christian charity, the reception of the Eucharist. The breaking of bread disappeared into the invisible fraction of the Host, overloaded with arcane symbolic significances but serving no purpose; the priest gobbled up the consecrated species himself; the people gazed but starved. The observation was certainly relevant to a population for whom the breaking of bread was a deeply ingrained ritual: just before the English peasants' revolt of 1381, a group of tenants of the Abbey of St Albans dug out an appropriately shaped millstone which the abbot had confiscated and cemented into the floor of the refectory, broke it up and each took home a piece.[11] The demand for the cup to be given to the laity which arose in Bohemia some thirty years later evidently throve on a sense of deprivation, though it does not seem to have aroused much sympathy elsewhere. A case could indeed be put for the contrary view: a lack of commensality was not the principal failing of traditional Christianity, and the rarity of communion gave it the solemnity of an annually recurring feast. Most parishes communicated only at Easter, though there were those who added Christmas and Pentecost to their statutory obligation. Communion needed to be prepared for by fasting and abstinence, by the forgiveness of sins in confession, and by giving some effect to the sentiments embodied in the *Pax*; it called for an extra offering, usually a penny; and it concluded with a parish feast. The usual time for this would be the end of Easter or Maundy Thursday mass. Communicants would normally receive wine as well as the Host, and though this was not consecrated except among the Bohemians, it was clearly something more solemn than the mouth-cleaning fluid the orthodox clergy felt obliged to pretend. Some miming of the gospel accounts of the Eucharist, like the Maundy Thursday feet-washing, would be common. Thereafter the parish, especially if it had a well-organized fraternity, might hope to sit down in the body of the church to a dinner of paschal lamb or something similar. Otherwise the priest would be expected to exercise himself in hospitality, though it would be a lucky parish that was treated to the kind of love-feast fixed up for his communicants by the English Benedictine Ambrose Barlow in seventeenth-century Lancashire.[12]

Historians have none the less usually held that the sacramental aspect of the pre-Reformation mass did not measure up to the sacrificial, that the parts were better accommodated than the whole. This is perhaps an optical illusion arising from the transference of much eucharistic feeling, especially in towns, where parochial community was often rather weak, away from the annual communion at Easter on to the brand-new feast of Corpus Christi. Invented in the thirteenth century, in time for Thomas Aquinas to write a liturgy for it, it did not become popular until towards the middle of the fourteenth. During the next two centuries it took on to an astonishing degree and frequently acquired the sort of primacy in the year suggested by the simple term which came to be used for it by the French, the *Fête-Dieu*. It fell ten days after Pentecost, and the reason given was that Maundy Thursday, coming in the middle of the most intense phase of the penitential season, was no time for a joyful feast. The pressure of penitential enthusiasm in Holy Week was certainly a relevant factor, but in the diffusion of Corpus Christi we are dealing with something like the anonymous working-out of an axiom of social theology expressed in ritual: that in a sequence of events intended to create unity, the representation of unity must come at the end. As at the beginning of the Middle Ages the kiss of peace had been moved from the beginning to the end of the mass, so at their close the feast of the Eucharist found a new place as the last of the great feasts commemorating the Redemption, the end of what has been called apropos of Coventry the public half of the ritual year. The classic representation of the social miracle in the closing Middle Ages, its theme was the reconciliation of the parts and the whole, the union of social limbs in the body of Christ, at a time when their normal conjunction might have been better represented by the body of More's or Shakespeare's Richard III. The theme was worked out in the office and mass of the feast, in the great procession where the sequence of crafts and orders led up to the Host carried under its canopy, in the series of verse plays which marked the stages of the procession and told the history of the world, integrating the disparate efforts of the gilds into a single whole. It was echoed in the neighbourhood conviviality of the evening, and indeed of the following day if, as at York, the plays expanded to fill the whole of the feast itself. The play of Corpus Christi, it has been suggested, meant more than the theatrical performance; it meant the event itself as a gratuitous release, a representation of *homo ludens* under the aegis of the Host. Invented as it may have been by priests and patricians, the feast of the body of Christ, divided but whole, eaten but never consumed, acquired an intense popular loyalty which ensured its survival through the contempt of humanists, the hatred of reformers and the puritanism of the orthodox. It also survived the efforts, which were frequent in the fifteenth century, to annex its symbolism to the benefit of kings and secular authorities. What undermined it in the end, as it undermined the *Pax*, was the rise among the devout of the piety of frequent communion: that intimate, interior, even mystical devotion to Christ present in the sacrament which a chorus of fifteenth-century masters as different as Thomas à Kempis and Savonarola was to bequeath to the Counter-Reformation and, in spite of itself, to the Reformation as well.

(iii) Deliverance

The salvation spoken of in the mass, as in the daily Christian greeting, was deliverance from the evils of this world as well as everlasting beatitude in the next. True, there were other conceptions of salvation. There was the Roman idea, cultivated by medieval emperors, that *salus* was the fruit of victory, and peace what happened when you had conquered the other side; and the usage of the people of Montaillou shows that there were numbers of quite ordinary people for whom salvation was strictly a matter of the eternal destiny of the soul. The English 'soul-hele (-health)' testifies to a sense of the necessary distinctions. But the first conception was bookish, and the second had to struggle with language, not least with the language of the Church, before it could be taken as understood.

Perhaps it is significant that there is not very much evidence of the cult of the saints in Montaillou. For the power to bring *salus* to the body—to cure, to restore, to make whole—had been from the beginning a sign of the restoration of amity in the universe to which they witnessed. As they became more humane, this power was conceived as a particular kind of skill, and their lives were scrutinised for clues to what that skill might be—the curing of sore throats or sick babies, the recovery of stolen or mislaid goods, and so on. When new causes of death and disintegration appeared, one looked harder at the details of the deaths of the martyrs, finding in St Sebastian, because of the multitude of his wounds, a protector against the plague, and in St Barbara, killed by a wrathful father and apparently for that reason a recourse in thunder and lightning, a shield against the dreadful effects of gunpowder. It should be said that in these cases salvation of the soul was also in question, for the formal object of prayer was to preserve the Christian from *sudden* death and so ensure that he would not go to his maker without the benefit of the last sacraments. By comparison with those of the heroic age, the saints were now more concerned with prevention than with cure, and their services were services of friendship rather than of power.

As well as to individuals, such protection was naturally owed by saints to the collectivities of which they were patrons, but we should avoid treating them as simply prisoners of their clientele. The saint would protect his parish or fraternity or country if duly honoured by it, and due honour meant that it should show itself a genuine Christian community; hence the patronal feast-day entailed, besides its formal observances, an effort on the part of the community to surpass itself in penitence and charity. The saint became a sort of metaphor for the social miracle on which exterior deliverances would depend. The signs are that this frame of mind was becoming more prevalent; or it may be that the parish, a comparatively recent invention, was only now establishing itself in people's feelings as an acceptable vehicle for it. It governed, at all events, the rogation ceremonies. As a rogation or rite of petition, this annual perambulation of the parish in early summer was an occasion when the priest prayed for and blessed the fields. As a procession, it was the ordered and visible progress of a whole community, carrying its banners against the forces of darkness, whose efficacy would be called in doubt if ill-tempered neighbours refused to join in: they quite often did. It governed most directly a favourite institution of rural Castile, the vow. Vows were widely undertaken by individuals, but this was a collective engagement, inspired by exterior disasters like plagues of locusts, to observe a feast-day, usually of a saint but never of the parish patron, in return for the averting or ending of the distress. By the late sixteenth century, when Philip II's bureaucracy decided that vows required investigation, their accumulation over the years had composed in most parishes a festal cycle which was individual to itself and more popular than the conventional one. Vowing the feast meant that on that day, annually, the population obliged itself to go to mass, possibly to receive the sacraments, often to fast on the vigil and sometimes on the day itself, but always to engage collectively in the rites of charity, whatever they might be; whence the occasions were known as *caridades*.

Not all the powers of exterior deliverance vested in the Church were examples of salvation through charity. Most of the remainder were derivatives of sacramental rituals, and so in some sense extensions of the social miracle; there were those in the early sixteenth century, like the preacher John Geiler, who in an increasingly hostile intellectual climate sought to defend them on these grounds. But it seems fair to say, about the two major categories of what would henceforth count as superstition, that one had its source in the miracle of charity and the other did not. The first category related to the Eucharist. It may be understood from the comment of the woman near Montaillou who said that if a man did not go to communion during epidemics or on feast-days there must be something wrong with him; or as a set of variations on the idea that while you were present at mass you did not grow older. Carried in procession at Corpus Christi or in face of emergent dangers of riot and fire, received by the dying, seen at the elevation in the mass, or (allegedly) sprinkled in powder form on caterpillars in the garden, the salutiferous effects of the Host seem mostly instances of the dogma of salvation by charity, healing by wholeness. In the other principal category of salutiferous effects, whose model was the rite of baptism, we are dealing with something else, salvation by exorcism. It included two universal remedies: holy water and the sign of the cross. Clearly, as in the case of sin, there was here an area of anxiety which the doctrine of the primacy of charity had failed to reduce; a region whose expansions and contractions may possibly count as a negative index of the hold of the gospel of Christ over a population of Christians. It is implausible, and insulting, to regard it as exhausting the religious emotions of traditional Christianity. We are not forced to believe that it was expanding in the century before the Reformation, though the history of baptism and marriage may suggest that it was doing so, and why. If I may risk another conjecture about the general opinion of the age, it is that charity would defend one against the wrath of God, but cunning and power were required against the machinations of the Devil, and probably against those of one's neighbour as well. The special virtue of the salutary Host was that it managed to offer a supreme representation of love and power at once.

5   Enemies of the Human Race

Christianitas, like the Christian, like the author of the psalms, was encompassed by enemies. One might have thought that the list of these would have been headed, in place of the Philistines, by the Muslims. The tradition of the crusade, though no longer what it had been, was still a reality; and there was no shortage of exterior confrontations in an age which witnessed the Islamisation of Constantinople and the Christianisation of Granada. It also witnessed the submersion of Greek and Balkan Christianity under the Ottomans, a continuing state of holy piracy and mutual enslavement kept up by Barbary corsairs and Knights of St John, and a Christian counter-offensive by the Portuguese which carried the conflict into Africa, the Indian Ocean and the East. From a public point of view Islam remained the prime enemy of Christendom, and emperors and popes regularly reminded it of the fact. But, for all that, the relations of Catholics with Moors rarely attained the degree of passion which attended their other hostilities, and this requires some explanation. Reasons may be found in the state of relations between Latin and Greek Christianity, which made Latins philosophical about the trials of the Greeks, just as Greeks, when driven to it, preferred the rule of the Turks to that of the Latins; and in the diet of romances of chivalry which gave large numbers of Christians the idea that all Muslims were gentlemen, a race of Saladins and Othellos. It remains, considering the rooted hostility which generally prevailed on the other side, a little hard to understand; and one can only suggest that for the development of a real Christian hatred, some further degree of ultimate intimacy or cultural relevance was required. What was lacking with Muslims, almost as much as with Mongols or Chinese, was a recognition of the self in the other which would evoke the dreadful truth that a man's enemies were of his own household.

Such, in the most obvious cases, were the usurer and the witch. 'Thou shalt not lend upon usury to thy brother', said

Deuteronomy; and whether or not this text was decisive for scholastic commentators, it was certainly the first consideration for the average Christian, as the statutes of any fraternity will demonstrate. From St Ambrose in the fifth century to San Bernardino in the fifteenth, preachers insisted that the taking of usury, or profit on the use of something lent, was an act of hostility and an offence against charity to one's neighbour. San Bernardino's course of Lenten sermons given in Siena in 1425 seems a classic exposition of the theme. He avoided much of the painful argumentation with which scholastics sought to rationalise the taboo for the benefit of business men, and affirmed the ideal that Christians should lend to one another freely, 'hoping for nothing in return', except that when they were in need themselves their neighbour should do the same for them. I cannot say how far this exhortation corresponded to the facts of daily life, but clearly it was idealistic to suppose that spontaneous free lending could have met all the temporal needs of Christians. Otherwise it would not have been necessary for the friars to agitate for the establishment of *monti di pietà*. These were designed to put the Jews out of business, and were extremely popular; they do not prove that there was no real taboo against usury, since usury was conceived as occurring in a relationship between individuals. As Shakespeare expounded the tradition in *The Merchant of Venice*, 'taking something more' in return for a loan was a breach of friendship, and he who took it from another while feigning friendship was actually a blood-enemy, as the plot would reveal. By contrast, the relation of surety or bond to debtor was one of sacrificial brotherhood, intensified by Shakespeare to a degree which makes it clear that Antonio's model is the Atonement of Christ as Anselm conceived it. Written in a climate of Elizabethan prudential scepticism, Shakespeare's treatment of the theme would seem to me, as to Benjamin Nelson, both a reworking of traditional ethics and an appeal to fundamental values which would be recognised as binding by his audience. Their memory might have been jogged by recent parliamentary debates, in which the sources and contemporary literature of the subject had been ventilated. Shakespeare probably did not know that the thesis about sureties had been contradicted by Luther, who otherwise shared his view of the subject. He and the audience are likely to have been aware that in taking such questions to touch (like incest) on areas of fundamental taboo he had against him the voice of humanistically educated opinion, which agreed with Calvin that usury could sometimes be a public benefit. Against these ultimate choices the struggles of scholastics with the niceties of *lucrum cessans* and *damnum emergens* seem comparatively small beer.

Shakespeare also wrote a play containing witches, and though his depiction of them might appeal to more modern tastes, it had a solid traditional core. By his time the witch had certainly replaced the usurer as an embodiment of malice, and it is hard to know whether she had been an object of equal popular concern in 1400. Witches, if their wrath was aroused and their techniques successful, afflicted one's body or children. They killed swine, spread sickness among cattle and turned their milk into blood. They smote one's sexual organs with impotence, and brought down storms to ruin one's crops. Occasionally (less in everyday life than in the stress of high political conflict) they persecuted unto death. They were workers of an inverted *salus*, 'noxious creatures undermining the health and welfare of their neighbours'. We need not be surprised that such creatures were thought, or thought themselves, to exist, in a universe where the physical domain was subject to the governance of the social, to wrath and love emanating from God or man, or from intermediate beings like saints and demons. And simple misogyny is not quite enough to explain why most witches were thought to be women. Women, particularly if old, unmarried and unfriended, were like monks, who resorted to exceptional methods in the pursuit of their quarrels because their calling forbade them to use conventional ones; they were vessels of a resentment otherwise impotent. Male witches were frequently, and for the same reason, members of the clergy. Where a man would proceed by fire and sword they proceeded by sickness and evil weather.

Although attempts have been made to fix her (or him) in space and time, the witch seems a universal stereotype of the Christian West, identical in rural England, in the mining regions of Germany, in Swiss or Pyrenean valleys, French or Italian cities. It has often seemed that fears about witchcraft, or the actual practice of it, were increasing from the late fourteenth century, and maybe the disasters of that period did have some sensitising effect. But the feeling is probably an illusion, arising from the extension of public judicial systems and a greater willingness to bring to court disputes where witchcraft was suspected. This was almost certainly the story through the fifteenth century.

The more sensational repercussions of the story will have to be postponed until later, since they cannot really be understood as part of the traditional universe. But something of significance was clearly going on during the decades after 1400, and there is a good deal to be learnt from trying to find out exactly what it was. One may describe it as a hardening conviction that witches were not merely individual enemies of individual Christians, but were connected in a general conspiracy aimed at the overthrow of Christendom as a whole. It would be a mistake to think that this suspicion had no spontaneous roots. One might assume that in the pursuit of pure malevolence witches, like those in *Macbeth*, would seek to maximise damage by collaborating with others of their kind, and not easily deny that behind each particular manifestation of malice one was to look for the hand of the universal fiend, the Devil. That witches were popularly supposed to form such a 'sect' of malice is clear from the language used to describe their offence in unsophisticated parts of Christendom like the alpine valleys, where they were thought especially common. It was 'Vauderie', or Waldensianism, something reminiscent of the groups of obstinate heretics who, in other alpine valleys and elsewhere, maintained their segregation from the Catholic community. For further elaborations of the theme the populace was indebted to the world of clerical learning, which had always, in order to support a more effective repression of it, sought to define witchcraft as an offence against faith. A decision in this sense of the theological faculty of Paris, published in 1395, seems to have marked a point of some importance. One of the important things about it was that it defined the offence not simply as apostasy but as idolatry. This was in the first place a consequence of viewing witchcraft as an offence against the first commandment, which theologians had commonly done; but it probably also had something to do with Gerson's opinion that ethics fell into the domain of faith, not of reason, which gave authority to the Old Testament conception of the witch as an idolater. The idea that witchcraft was an offence in 'religion', superimposed on the suspicion that witches formed a sect, warranted the conclusion that in the proceedings of witches the Devil was not just a manager of maleficent activity but an object of worship. You only had to know true worship to imagine what perversities the worship of the Devil might entail. From some such conflation of popular and learned themes emerged the lurid exposé of the doings of witches published with papal approval by the Dominicans Jakob Sprenger and Heinrich Krämer in the 1480s, the *Malleus maleficarum* or *Hammer of the Witches*. Thereafter the shadowy witches' synagogue of the fourteenth century passed into the sabbath of the sixteenth, and the malicious neighbour into the 'adversary of a broader and less personal society', the enemy of the human race.

It is understandable that witches were held to form a sect, since the sect was the type of dissidence with which the orthodox were best acquainted. They were not necessarily much acquainted with it at all, for he would have been an excessively hopeful (or fearful) observer who would have thought such dissidence on the increase during the fifteenth century. There is a good deal in the theory that the Church's machinery of repression took up the persecution of spurious heretics because, in view of the lack of real ones, it would otherwise have found time lying heavy on its hands. The most formidable rivals of medieval orthodoxy, the ultra-puritan Cathars of the south, had been extirpated with a comprehensiveness which must reflect internal exhaustion as well as exterior pressure; and it is difficult to be sure how much the evangelical sectarianism of the Waldensians survived outside its enclaves in the western Alps. These remained, however, something of a model for others in their withdrawal from the complexities and compromises of a Church open to all, in order to cultivate something more instantly recognisable as a community of the gospel. It is generally held that this was, at least in the long run, the character of English Lollardy. Though its early phases were dominated by John Wyclif, a figure from the milieu of professional theology and establishment politics, it did not long retain, if it had entertained at any time, an ambition to reconstruct the 'universal' Church. In the light of Wyclif's doctrine that the Church was not the visible and reassuringly comprehensive community which Catholics assumed, but a ghostly diaspora of the predestined, it is not easy to see how it could have done. It looks as if the natural environments of Lollards were the privacies of the chaplain-keeping nobility and of the respectable artisan or peasant. They conducted from their retreats a cult of the Bible considered less as a medium of instruction or spiritual experience than as a transmissible symbol of superior sanctity, and of the Ten Commandments as a law against saints and images. They pursued a campaign of denigration, high-minded or vulgar, of the sacramental and social rites which formed the nexus of the Christianity of the average soul. Although they included priests, some of them parish priests, they did not manage to extract from Wyclif any positive doctrine of the Eucharist. They seem to have had hankerings after the commemorative idea of the Lord's Supper which was later to be associated with Zwingli, but made no apparent effort to embody it in practice; they preferred to go to church, if only to scoff at their neighbours. Like such people at most times, they were unpopular, and it remains an open question what, if anything, they contributed to English Protestantism.

In their concern for the Eucharist the Hussites, the only major dissidents of the fifteenth century, differed from their precursors. John Hus was a vernacular preacher in an age of vernacular preachers, whose vernacular happened to be Czech. He was also, like Wyclif, a secular priest when such preachers were usually friars. These disadvantages led to the accusation, false by his own account, that he was a disciple of Wyclif. As such as he was condemned to be burned in 1415 by the Fathers of the Council of Constance, who were preoccupied with organising the unity of the Church. Whether or not Hus was a Wycliffite, the Hussites were certainly no Lollards: they stood for the collective salvation of the Czech people by a public repression of sin and a more intense cultivation of the Eucharist, which finally took the form of universal communion in both kinds (*utraque specie*). Known for this reason as Utraquists, they were about as radical as Joan of Arc, and their backbone was a pious nobility. The outward face of their solidarity was an extreme hostility to Bohemian Germans and, after the burning of Hus, to the orthodox Church as a whole, which had brought upon the Czech nation a dishonour requiring to be avenged. If we discount the partisanship characteristic of the time, their deviance was hardly more than a creative elaboration of the themes of mainstream Catholicism; it might have been handled more sensitively if the higher instances of the Church had not been, when it occurred, in the throes of trying to end the Great Schism. Perhaps they were also suffering from the general hardening of the arteries which is commonly alleged. Once the Czechs' ambition to create for themselves a distinctive community within the Church universal had been so brusquely repudiated, and the guiding figures of the Church had placed it in the camp of their enemies, it was fairly inevitable that something drastic would happen.

What happened among the Czech rank and file was the millenarian reaction that the passing of the Church into the hands of the enemy was an unmistakable prophetic sign of the impending second coming of Christ. Under that great shadow it behoved the friends of God to fuse their separate selves in the perfect brotherhood which required the abolition of mine and thine and of conventional hierarchies of rank; to preach universal kinship and universal community; and to exterminate with the sword of righteousness all who stood in their way. The Czechs did not need to invent these ideas, since the moral system of medieval Christianity was guaranteed to inspire them from time to time. What they had to find was someone to put them into effect, since the conventional vehicle of wrath was the Christian Emperor, and the available emperor-figure, Sigismund King of the Romans, was their chief enemy. They solved their problem by invoking the personal leadership of Christ. True, Christ did not turn up in February 1420 on the mountain which they had named in anticipation Mount Tabor. But they came down from the mountain a formidable host, for a decade or more the chief military power in central and eastern Europe, and a nightmare to the orthodox, the conventional and the Germans. The exigences of actual warfare may have undermined the convictions for which the Taborites had entered upon it, but these remained strong enough to see them through a crushing defeat in 1434 to the final destruction of their sanctuary in 1452. Meanwhile the pious Utraquists, their honour vindicated, were doing their best to come to a settlement with the rest of the Church; but although a formal agreement was reached the papacy proved unwilling to implement it, and by the middle of the century the Bohemian Church had fallen into a sad condition of decay and disarray.

Millenarian ideas succeeded before the end of the century in implanting themselves in orthodox Saxony, where they would be heard of again at the time of the Reformation. But in Bohemia itself they died out, leaving the field to a body which maintained the ideals of the movement for the individual or group, but abandoned them for the population at large. The Unity of Brothers, which defined itself as a separate Church in 1467, was the last spontaneous offshoot of pre-Reformation Christianity, and is worthy on that score of more attention than it usually receives. Its position in the Christianity of fifteenth-century Bohemia was much that of the Quakers in seventeenth-century England. Like the Quakers, it emerged out of a separatist tradition and rejected the formal structures of Church, State and social hierarchy as Christian institutions. In this it was no doubt indebted to the Wycliffite and Waldensian influences which are visible in the ideas of their principal inspirer, Peter Chelčicky; he had added to them a rigorous aversion to the idea, as the Taborites had embodied it, of erecting a Christian community by warfare. But these influences seem to account only for the form of the Unity, not for its content, which remained distinctly traditional; this was true of its understanding of the sacraments and of the idea of fraternity itself. As well as renouncing and rejecting warfare among Christians, the Brothers rejected litigation in law-courts, and held that disputes ought to be settled by brotherly arbitration and restitution; where this was not feasible, they demanded exterior penance from the guilty party, to be accepted by the party offended as an adequate ground for reconciliation. Above all operations of the secular law, they resisted the *judicium sanguinis* or death penalty, as leaving no possibility for the Christian reconciliation of offences. For the same reason they rejected the Old Testament as a moral authority. In their cultivation of the Christian figure of the peasant, and consequent hostility to noblemen, they seem closer to William Langland than to Thomas Muentzer and the peasants of the German Peasants' War two generations later, and would have dismissed as Luther did their claim to constitute a Christian *Gemeinschaft*. Their fraternal ethos proved attractive outside Bohemia, and was something of a model for the milder Anabaptists; in a watered-down form it established itself as a permanent feature of Christianity in central Europe. Though they could probably not have been integrated into any comprehensive church, utraquist or catholic, they seem in themselves not dissidents from traditional Christianity but representatives of what was most attractive in it. Excepting that the segregation of Bohemia preserved them from confrontation with the powers of institutional Catholicism, they illustrate well the thesis that most of the heresies of the late Middle Ages were effervescences of orthodoxy defined into exclusion by an unimaginative establishment.

Amongst all those who were consigned by conventional

Christians to the category of enemies of the human race the most unquestionable were the Jews. The difference of attitude to Jews and to Muslims is unmistakable, and cannot be ascribed either to the possession in the one case, and absence in the other, of the power of forcible retaliation; nor yet to the exercise by Jews of financial pressure on the Christian population, which has tempted historians to treat their hostilities as an episode of class war. The Jews were not a class but a people, and if they were often engaged in money-lending and tax-collection among Christians this was a self-fulfilling effect of a previous antagonism. The peculiarly intense character of this hostility, both in the population and among the learned from Ramon Lull in the thirteenth century to Luther in the sixteenth, does not require exotic explanation. The Jews were the original enemies of Christ, who had procured his crucifixion and death and had taken his blood upon their heads and upon those of their children. Nothing was easier for the average Christian to understand than that this was a crime which cried out for vengeance, and the more the events of Christ's human history, above all the Incarnation and the Passion, became objects of the popular imagination, the more lurid the colours in which was painted the inexhaustible malice of the Jews.

It was an obvious effect of the popular mission of the friars to instil this rider to the Anselmian story of the Redemption into a population only too ready to receive it. It was propagated by the Catalan Dominican Vicent Ferrer, who died in 1419 and was canonised in 1455, and by a string of his disciples, who included Bernardino of Siena. I should be surprised if they were not conscious that their campaign for the reconciliation of enmities among Christians would be furthered by proposing to the population an outlet for legitimate hatred. Thus for Jewish communities clustered precariously around their synagogues from Frankfurt to Seville, however much they might be assured of the benevolence of kings and civic authorities, the time of the preaching of penance was always a time of danger. At Carnival in Rome they were required to display themselves publicly, like other instruments of the Devil, running races through the streets under streams of abuse or whips, and held up to derision or contempt on the stage. These occasions seems relatively good-natured by comparison with those of the Spanish kingdoms, where it was fairly common for the preaching and representation of the Passion in Holy Week to culminate in a riot against the Jewish quarter, or at best in a collective refusal to sell food to Jews in the hope of starving them to death. The association of German Passion plays with anti-Semitism is a well-known theme, though these do not seem to have preceded the Reformation. As self-determined objects of divine vengeance, Jews were understood to expose to the same vengeance all who communicated with them: hence the widely held doctrine that physical contact with them entailed pollution, and the consequent taboo not merely against intermarriage but against the touching by Jews of food or other goods in the market-place. The taboo extending to prostitutes (as well as to public executioners), it was often thought economical or witty, as in Frankfurt, to situate the brothels in the *Judengasse*. In this state of public emotions, the instant reaction to a major visitation of divine wrath on any town which harboured Jews was to attack them and purge it by expulsion, fire or massacre. The passage of the Black Death left a train of shattered Jewish communities across the Rhineland and southern Germany; the more intricate defences of the Iberian Jews protected them from disaster until 1391, but when it came it was the more comprehensive for that. The difference here was that kings were persuaded to divert the will to exterminate into a policy of forcible conversion, so transforming (in appearance) a problem about Jews into a problem about heretics, which was to dog them for a century and more.

No one will wish to underestimate the reality of the *convivencia*, or living side by side of people of different 'laws', which was a distinctive feature of medieval Iberian and, to some extent, of Italian society. In many respects their communities of Jews might be considered as corporate entities or *universitates* participating with the multitude of other such autonomous corporations in the segmental structure of the traditional social universe. A synagogue was not much more out of place in Venice than the neighbourhood church of a noble *gens* in Genoa; and like such *gentes* Jews occupied their own quarter, in the first place, out of preference and solidarity. They might also, from time to time, participate in communal life by appearing at mass or contributing to collective prayers or shows. But where the definition of community was ultimately the mystical body of Christ they were in the end unassimilable members or cancerous growths, and the more the doctrine became absorbed by the Christian masses the more it seemed to become urgent that the growth be cut out. From the fourteenth century a coalition of friars and population relentlessly pressed upon the authorities a policy of formal segregation, the wearing by Jews of distinctive marks, and other humiliations; in Italy the pressure took the form of a general agitation for the establishment of *monti di pietà*, which would deprive Jews of their most obvious function and means of livelihood, as well as of their ability to exercise malice against Christians. Luther inherited something from both sides of this coalition, and returned in his mature years to an exacerbated version of the tradition he had seemed in his reforming idealism to be going to abandon. In the end, he concluded, the problem about Jews was a problem about race, and against their own intransigent racialism it was useless to nurture the Christian hope of creating by conversion a community of the reborn in which there would be neither Jew nor Greek. They were enemies of Christ and of Christians; unlike witches, there seemed to be no scriptural warrant for exterminating them, but their houses and synagogues should be burned down and the race, if not expelled from Christian lands, enslaved. On this point Luther was at one with the popes who, contrary to the historic attitude of the papacy, issued bulls to the same effect at much the same time. In neither case did they quite carry respectable opinion with them, but under such auspices the sixteenth century, in Germany and Italy alike, became the century of the ghetto.

Meanwhile in the Spanish kingdoms, now progressing from baffling diversity towards imperfect unity, the traumatic denouement of centuries of precarious *convivencia* had already occurred. Luther's allegation that racialism was a peculiar property of Jews, though not exactly false, was hardly fair to the history of the Peninsula during the fifteenth century; like his contemporary Gianpietro Carafa (Pope Paul IV), he knew enough about that to give publicity, when political hostilities suggested it, to the idea that all Spaniards were half-Jews anyway. If one were looking for signs of an exhaustion of the genuine Christian impulse during the fifteenth century, a preoccupation with lineage and blood, a falling-back from the kith to the kin, from the community of the Eucharist to the community of the caste or the rites of passage, would certainly be one of them. They are most apparent in the history of Spain, or perhaps one should say of Castile. A century after the baptisms of 1391, the conviction of Old Christians had hardened that Judaism was a disease for which there was no cure, and the body of *conversos* a Trojan horse within the city, preparing the destruction of Christendom. On this conviction the Spanish Inquisition was founded in 1479; it guided the activity of Queen Isabella's right-hand man, Ximénez de Cisneros, and defeated the Christian universalism of the first Catholic archbishop of conquered Granada, Hernando de Talavera. A decade which elsewhere saw the official exposition of the new heresy of diabolic witchcraft concluded in Castile with the revelation of the story of the Holy Child of La Guardia, a projection in which all the fears and hatreds of late medieval Catholicism were compounded. In a small town near Ávila, a coven of unidentified Jews and *conversos* had murdered a Christian child, whose identity was equally obscure but who was evidently the child Jesus. They had crucified him, ritually insulted him, and finally cut out his heart and elevated it, like the Host, in the sight of their congregation. It was not clear that they had consumed the heart, but they—or no doubt the *conversos* among them, for whom nothing was easier—had procured genuine hosts which after being subjected to unmentionable indignities at the ritual had been, like the *viaticum* of the dying, distributed to confederates far and wide. The hosts would be kept by the *conversos* as talismans against the godly activities of the Inquisition, and used by the Jews to annihilate the Christian population by infecting it with rabies. The structure of an entire civilisation testified to the absolute plausibility of this event. In its aftermath the Jews of the Peninsula were destined to a further diaspora, and those among the *conversos* who survived the Inquisition to a distinguished part in the history of sixteenth-century Catholicism.

PART TWO

Christianity Translated

6 The Father, the Word and the Spirit

Something important happened to Western Christianity in the sixteenth century, and the term 'Reformation' is probably as good a guide as any to investigating what it was; I certainly have no superior alternative to propose. Yet it seems worth trying to use it as sparingly as possible, not simply because it goes along too easily with the notion that a bad form of Christianity was being replaced by a good one, but because it sits awkwardly across the subject without directing one's attention anywhere in particular. Properly speaking, it is a term from the vocabulary of ecclesiastical discipline, and means the restoration to some ideal norm, by the action of superiors, of the conduct of institutions and persons. It may be a necessary concept in the history of the Church as an institution; but it does not seem much use in the history of Christianity, since it is too high-flown to cope with actual social behaviour, and not high-flown enough to deal sensitively with thought, feeling, or culture. On the assumption that thought cannot be reformed, but minds may change, I start as before by exploring whether, in the instinctive understanding of Christianity, there existed for the sixteenth century axioms which went without saying.

(i) The Justice of God

Perhaps it will not seem credible to present Martin Luther as the voice of anonymous events, but the view can be defended. At the age of 31, when he began in Wittenberg his lecture-course on St Paul's Epistle to the Romans, he was a successful professor of theology in the tradition of the schools; he was also a careful observer of the pieties of his Augustinian order and of the exuberant Christianity around him. During the next nine months he expounded the doctrine of justification by faith as, under the guidance of Augustine and Bernard, he found it in St Paul, without giving his students, his superiors or himself any reason to doubt that he was a loyal, though unusually interesting, representative of scholastic tradition. A year or so later he composed ninety-five theses on indulgences. In these he recorded some problems theologians had been having about papal practice, with a view to maintaining the integrity of sacramental satisfaction, and in general of penitential conduct modelled on the sufferings of Christ, as a necessary item in the forgiveness of sins. Apart from a condemnation by the papacy, mainly because Pope Leo X's theologians were Dominicans who took a higher view of nature than Augustinians did, Luther's history during the next four years, which ended with his formal dissidence at the Reichstag at Worms in 1521, was governed by the dawning conviction that these two positions were incompatible. He abandoned the doctrine about satisfaction for the doctrine about justification. Luther was not a textual scholar, and on the whole resisted the contemporary tendency to find in textual scholarship the answer to all theological problems; but one piece of scholarship seems to have been particularly influential in persuading him to this conclusion. Erasmus's critical edition and retranslation of the New Testament had come out while he was lecturing on Romans, and during his leisure in the Saxon castle of the Wartburg after his retirement from Worms he was to translate it into German. Its first and perhaps major surprise was the proof, borrowed from the fifteenth-century classicist Lorenzo Valla, that where John the Baptist had been understood to be telling the Jews to do penance, or perform penitential acts, he had actually been telling them simply to change their minds (*metanoeite*). For the sixteenth century the reading of penance as *metanoia*, or conversion, carried the sort of absolute self-evidence which Anselm's doctrine of the Atonement had possessed five centuries before. It seems to have persuaded Luther that the idea of satisfaction for sin which Erasmus thought uncivilised was actually against the gospel, and that all forms of penitential or compensatory behaviour were to be identified with the 'works' St Paul had disparaged as a contribution to righteousness. In saying that we were justified through faith alone, or by gratuitously given grace received in a state of unstriving trust in God's mercy, he was in the first place telling his contemporaries that atonement and satisfaction were irrelevant to their reconciliation with God; or that, if they thought God could be appeased by the kinds of procedure which ought to satisfy their neighbours, they were mistaken.

Unlike Anselm's, Luther's thought did not start from a puzzle about the relation, within the godhead, between the Father and the redeeming Son, and it is not absolutely clear that he thought he disagreed with Anselm's solution. In fact he did, the victim, one may think, of something happening to language. He continued to speak of the satisfaction of the wrath of the Father by Christ's Passion and death, and indeed his dismissal of other kinds of satisfaction had the effect of a more relentless concentration on the sufferings of Christ crucified. But he did not mean what Anselm meant by satisfaction, and it has been suggested that he only used the word to avoid baffling the common man more than he had done already. What in Anselm had been an offer of compensation adequate to turn away due vengeance and restore amicable relations between offended God and offending man was taken by Luther as a submission to the punishment required by a criminal offence of public character. In Luther's penal or criminal theory of the Atonement, there was no transaction; the parties were not reconciled in the sense entailed by the English word, that two should become one, since the act was purely one-sided. There was no natural or social axiom to explain God's accepting Christ as a substitute for man in general, which in Anselm's theory was explained by kinship; it remained an impenetrable decision.

What in Luther seems to have been an effect of something like intellectual sleep-walking, or of a panic brought on by contemplation of a system of divine justice which had suddenly acquired a fearsome inflexibility, in his followers Melanchthon and Calvin emerged as a clear and distinct idea. Philip Melanchthon, an early convert from literary humanism who devoted his life to tidying Luther up, formulated it precisely as the doctrine of 'forensic' justification. Calvin, who knew more than Luther about the terrestrial legal system under which Christ was executed, used his talents to portray the application to Christ of penalties designed to punish 'thieves and other wrongdoers' and to evoke the agony in which, on the cross, he felt himself finally judged by his Father and 'suffered in his soul the terrible torments of a condemned and forsaken man' (*The Institutes*, II. xvi–xvii). In this version of the doctrine of the descent into hell, Calvin was applying to divine justice the modernised analogy of law which Luther had darkly perceived, in rather the way that Luther's mystery of reconciliation with God became in his hands the doctrine of predestination. In the next century the analogy was to be worked out in some detail by the Dutch jurist Hugo Grotius.

For a social historian the striking character of the new doctrine of the Atonement is its rejection of the event from the field of social relationships, the deprivation, in deference to what was not quite a necessary reading of St Paul, of its character of an equitable and objective exchange. That so important a revision should have occurred without in itself giving rise to any controversy—except with those who took the view that Christ's death was purely a moral example—is a testimony to the power of unconscious changes even over a generation of intellects as creative and self-conscious as those of the early sixteenth century. Concealed in the Lutheran preaching of justification by faith alone, or later in the Calvinist message that the business of the Christian life was not reconciliation with God but obedience to his sovereign will, it carried instantaneous conviction. By collapsing their foundations it demolished at a stroke whole wings of the edifice of contemporary piety.

It became less urgent to prove, at least in the way that it had hitherto seemed necessary, the absolute humanity of Christ. It has been generally held that Reformation theologians saw Christ as redeeming more by virtue of his godhead than of his manhood. The point has been difficult to expound to general satisfaction, but some idea of it may be conveyed by the contrast that in Anselm Christ the man offered his godhead as compensation, whereas in Reformation theology Christ as God consigned his manhood to penal punishment. Calvin certainly spent a lot of time in the *Institutes* confuting a view of some other reformers, that justification was given to man solely by Christ as a divine person, as incompatible with any form of the doctrine of Atonement. But he also had burned the Spanish intellectual refugee Miguel Servetus for holding that the revival of true Christianity depended on shedding the idea of the divinity of Christ. His final position was that while the defeat of the human Christ on the cross had wiped the human slate of sin, the restoration of positive righteousness was to be attributed to the victory of the divine Christ manifested in the Resurrection. Though they were in obvious ways indebted, Luther in particular, to the model of the suffering Christ dear to their immediate predecessors, the Christ of the reformers was in the end a *Christus victor* who had something in common with the Christ of Michelangelo's *Last Judgement*, and even of baroque Catholicism.

There were scholarly reasons for casting off the web of human relationships which pre-Reformation *pietas* had spun around the figure of Christ; but they drew their force from the revision which deprived Christ's kinship to man of its status as a necessary axiom of reason in the story of the Redemption. The multifarious kindred of St Anne would no longer be an absorbing object of contemplation; devotion to Christ's mother as the locus of universal reconciliation would be taken as an idolatrous detraction from the single-handed victory of her son; enthusiasm for Christmas would be widely viewed as jumping the gun, a premature celebration of peace on earth. Not indeed by all reformers: Luther, like Erasmus with his devotion to Our Lady of Loreto, was clearly in the line of the fifteenth-century inventors of a domesticated Holy Family, though this was for both of them rather less an essential link in the chain of salvation, rather more a model for human imitation. They probably had the best of it in the long run. But Calvin was more representative of the immediate Reformation mood in his dismissal of the whole complex as a tiresome if not suspect irrelevance. The Holy Family scarcely made an appearance in the *Institutes,* and it seems in accordance with his intentions that his English followers should have wished to abolish Christmas.

In most places the first visible sign that a drastic reconstruction of Christianity was under way was a casting-off of the saints. It took the form of a systematic vandalising of their images in canvas, wood and stone undertaken by a public authority, a mob to which reformed Christianity had been preached, or a combination of both. Where this was not simple philistinism, it represented a protest against the humanisation of the social universe effected in traditional belief by the reconciliation of man and God. In so far as the saints were God's friends by natural kinship, they were otiose or mythological. If they were thought to have achieved that friendship by meritorious sacrifice, and to be in a position to communicate their merit to others, they were a testimony to a mistaken theory of salvation. So inconceivable to the educated of the reformers' generation was the concept of merit, that Calvin was hard put to it to defend the view that Christ had acquired any merit by his unspeakable sufferings. So much less the saints. Fearful of seeing another crop of merit grow out of the ashes of the old, he instructed the chroniclers of Catholic persecution to avoid the terms 'saint' and 'martyr' in the description of its victims. This was admittedly more than human nature could bear. The leaders of the orgy of image-smashing which occurred in August 1566 in the Netherlands, the heartland of late medieval iconology, contrasted the living saints burned by their enemies with the dumb idols demolished by themselves. English and French Protestants cherished their martyrs.

Hence, although the Reformation attitude to saints and their images was often unduly dependent on Old Testament examples and injunctions, and seemed to exemplify the propitiation of an irritably jealous God which Reformation preachers were claiming to get rid of, it had roots in the conception of the singularity of Christ as redeemer. It was also, in a cruder way, a work of Christianity in that the emotions which accompanied it were those of people who had undergone some kind of traumatic conversion from a powerful conviction they had hitherto shared. As has been said of the Germans, the image-breakers had previously been image-makers. In its long history the relationship with the saints had encompassed fear and aggression as well as love and respect; the intensely personal tone of traditional devotion probably carried within itself the prospect of an equally intense reaction, once the news had got around that the saints were unable to meet their obligations in this world or the next. Thomas More detected personal hatred beneath the early reformers' talk about idolatry, and would not have been surprised by the mutilation, eye-gouging, face-battering, decapitation and gibbeting to which the statues in Netherlands churches, including those of Christ, were subjected in 1566. This was a back-handed proof of what the reformers had always contended, that people took the statue for the saint himself. Anxiety, Calvin said, was the reason why people had sought the saints' intercession in the first place, but there was the same anxiety in their destruction, a foretaste of the emotions of the witch-craze. In this case, it is true, anxiety was easier to allay. God's unwillingness to avenge his alleged friends, and their incapacity to avenge themselves, could be taken as established no later than the morning after.

Rome certainly learnt the lesson, and took some time to recover its nerve. When it did, it adopted the humanist notion that a saint was a model of virtue rather than a friend or benefactor, and presented heroic figures for public wonder or imitation, not for private affection. The large gestures of the baroque saint were made towards an audience of thousands, not to the kneeling donor or the old woman lighting her candle. Renaissance taste, and possibly the fear that people would take the image for the saint, inhibited experiments in a more demotic mode, which seem themselves a little too self-conscious. Bernini's ecstatic St Teresa was too far gone to inspire intimacy or reciprocity; Caravaggio's dead Virgin too close for comfort. The millions mostly lived on their devotional capital until the Sacred Heart triumphed in the teeth of Rome in the eighteenth century. This, like the domestic Holy Family, had actually been invented in the fifteenth.

Distaste for such images of all-too-human *pietà* must be something to do with the idea of the unfettered sovereignty of God, to whom alone a Christian piety should be directed. One might have illustrated the same effect from the fate of the souls in purgatory, suddenly no longer an object of obsessive human concern but an affront to the power or mercy of God. The instant dissolution of the multitude of relationships tradition had fostered, as having nothing to do with the salvation of the soul, let alone with the health of the body, was an extraordinary event in the history of Christianity and surely of human society at large. I doubt if we have really measured its consequences. I am not sure that it liberated people from the past in any way that one would want to be liberated from it. But there is something to be said for the idea that the dismantling of a social edifice existing in a perpetual present sharpened anxiety for a congenial past and future.

(ii) The Word

'In the beginning was the Word.' No doubt we should give primacy among the anonymous forces of change to a devaluation of image and symbol in favour of the audible or visible word; it was also a devaluation of the collective existence represented by sacraments, saints, and the 'unwritten' tradition of the Church, in favour of a naked confrontation with the scriptures. Two offspring of fifteenth-century Catholicism exemplify this shift. Around 1450 it had bred the printing-press in Mainz; in the 1460s it had bred Erasmus in Rotterdam. By 1500 each of them had matured sufficiently to begin to impose their mark on the culture of Christendom. In his relation to traditional Christianity Erasmus united a warm assent to its final objects with a perfect contempt for the way it had gone about trying to attain them. Peace, concord, reconciliation—between man and himself, man and man, man and God—remained the message of Christ; but satisfactions, penances, sacraments and rituals were no way to achieve any of them. They came by eloquent teaching and moral suasion, and issued in a frame of mind called *pietas,* a civilised devotion entailing the dominance of the spirit over the lusts of the flesh, the instincts of kinship and party, and the alleged physical or social incarnations of the holy. In the long run his deepest impact on the West was probably to supplant in daily life the rituals of Christianity by the rituals of civility; to the sixteenth century his Christian humanism or humanist Christianity meant above all the erection of classically inspired eloquence as a model for communication between God and man, and between men and each other. God's eloquence was principally contained in what he called the New Instrument, as his rendering of the beginning of St John's gospel explained: 'In principio erat sermo.' Once this critical tool was in the study of the scholar, and its message had been distilled for the unlearned, as in England, in handy volumes of précis distributed to churches, it would be the office of the 'ecclesiast' (hitherto priest) to retransmit it by the eloquence of his *sermo,* delivered as a living word to the *ecclesia* (assembly, congregation).

This was an exciting vision, designed to appeal to intellectuals brought up on the purified literary scholarship now being everywhere imported from Italy. It appealed to Luther, who had not been so brought up, and for a while he changed his name to the pseudo-classical Eleutherius and called himself an ecclesiast. He found its contents heady too, as in the abolition of penance by retranslation; and somewhere lurking in the doctrine of the primacy of faith is the classical understanding of *fides* as the feeling of conviction which the orator was supposed to arouse in his audience. His enthusiasm did not last, part of the difficulty being that Luther was an actual preacher, which Erasmus could never have been; for all his exaltation of the living *sermo,* and willingness to instruct others how to deliver it, his own eloquence lay irredeemably upon the printed page. To exactly which word the Christian community of the sixteenth century was being tuned is a question of some delicacy.

Erasmus himself is surely sufficient evidence that the 'word' of the sixteenth century was to a large extent the devocalised and desocialised medium whose emergence has been argued for by transatlantic media-theorists in the wake of Marshall McLuhan. William Tyndale, an English Erasmian who became Luther's first translator, was both an artist and a theologian of print; his argument with Thomas More over his English New Testament of 1525, which occupied the decade before they were both executed by their secular authorities, is a tes.imony to some such shift, and to the depth of the question raised. For Tyndale 'that word' which was in the beginning with God, which was the life and light of men and shone in uncomprehending darkness, was not a personal but a literal word; it was 'it', not 'him', instinctively conceived as the word written. It was certainly not the ritual word, for which traditional opinion seems sometimes to have taken it, but the vehicle of truth; and not the social word, but objective, transcendent, addressed to no one and everyone, like the Ten Commandments which were to replace statues and images behind the altars of English churches. For More it had no such primacy, being an imperfect method of communicating what could in principle be more exactly conveyed in images; the comic possibilities of this view were exploited by Rabelais in *Pantagruel* (II. xviii). The natural word oiled the wheels of human intercourse, told stories, made promises; the supernatural word was a web spun within the unbroken community of Christian people. It was the deposit, not the creator, of a common history, and in its written form neither the original, the only, nor the most important such deposit. Apart from the tradition of the Fathers, there were common custom, and the symbolic and sacramental mysteries; these were beyond and above language, not as for Tyndale suspect receptacles for the word, spreading damnation wherever their 'signification' was not verbally explicated and grasped.

It is fair to say that More's and Tyndale's respective valuations of the word were pretty exactly represented in the conduct of their arguments: in printed controversy the apostle of the word had an unfair advantage, which no doubt helped to persuade the martyrologist John Foxe that the art of printing had been providentially found out in time to forward the Reformation. Clearly the emergence of the Bible as a continuous text, in the vernacular and in print, was an event of radical importance to which Catholics found it difficult to adjust. A Catholic humanist like Reginald Pole found the stress of reconciling a textual scripturalism with the collective authority of the Church impossible to surmount; the Fathers of Trent rejected both his view of the scriptural doctrine of justification, which was the same as Luther's, and his attempt to rethink tradition as a continuum of Christian experience. Seeking to construct a defence of tradition against the onset of scriptural-ism, they proved incapable of putting the issue with More's sophistication, and fell back on a notion of tradition as a corpus of authoritative texts additional to scripture. They also initiated the process which turned the Vulgate into a text as absolute as any of the more scholarly versions favoured by reformers, and the liturgy itself began to suffer from typographical arthritis. It was not until the seventeenth century, as Catholics recovered their nerve and the progress of scholarship began to reveal the insecurity of 'ink-divinity', that a view of tradition could be formulated in which the collective historical experience of Christians was represented. By that time More's social miracle had become a pedagogical handing-down from father to son of the theorems of a Cartesian geometry, a state in which it was to continue until the Romantic revival.

So far we are bound to agree that the printing-press, though invented by German Catholics in the autumn of the Middle Ages, was a father of the Reformation, and of much else in the history of sixteenth-century Christianity. But simplified statements like Walter Ong's about the word 'moving from sound into space' depend on a misunderstanding of what was meant by reading. Until the seventeenth century silent reading was either an accomplishment of scholars or a self-conscious devotional mode. Reading meant muttering to oneself, or reading aloud to others: the written word was a 'hearable sign'. This was what it meant to the scripture-reading underground of English Lollardy, and also what it meant to Luther. His word was a word to be heard, a promise to be received in faith, not a text to be pored over. Faith, as St Paul had said, came by hearing; the ear, not the eye, was the Christian sense. This was common doctrine for reformers, and English Puritans were particularly strong on the theme. True, they were not keen on what they called 'reading', meaning the recitation of prescribed texts to a passive audience. Their mode was a plain version of the *theologia sermocinalis* preached by Erasmus and before him by fifteenth-century enemies of scholasticism like Nicholas of Cusa, where the text served as motto to a work of expository or hortatory art. Like Tyndale's, their word was creative of the community of true hearers, the Church; the press was a valuable auxiliary medium, not the master of the game.

Indeed, if we are looking for a typographical *pietas* practised by silent readers, we are more likely to find it among devout sixteenth-century Catholics, reading spiritual books in their pews and closets, than in the ranks of the reformed. For them the pious scriptoria of the Netherlands, and in its turn the press, had created an intimate version of monastic devotion which promoted individual meditation, silent prayer and interior dialogue with Christ in the sacrament or otherwise. Thomas à Kempis's *Imitation of Christ* was its best seller, and it was much encouraged by the relation of the Catholic and his confessor: Erasmus believed that the reading of such books ought to be encouraged instead of traditional satisfaction. To the government of King Henry VIII, such silent readers were examples of true religion, unlike the social scripture-readers who smelt of Lollardy and ought, if allowed at all, to be tolerated only among the gentry. True, the classic of the genre, Ignatius Loyola's *Spiritual Exercises*, was positively anti-typographical in character, a guide to the private communication of souls which followed More's opinion that the word was the servant of the mental image. But its substance was popularised outside the Society of Jesus by a mass of devotional paperbacks, and borrowed and adapted by reformers, at least in England, while they awaited the emergence of devotional writers of their own.

Perhaps in the end typography caught up with them all, imposing a Christianity of the text which none of those mentioned, except perhaps Tyndale, had originally intended. It caught up with Luther by way of the catechisms and Confessions into which his anarchic intuitions were regimented, as Melanchthon brought up his rear with the horses of instruction. Even so vocal a performance as his table talk, scribbled down among the dishes by devoted students, ended up as a textbook, its conversational crudities retouched. In so far as typography had not already caught up with More, it certainly caught up with the Elizabethan Catholics. In attempting to represent in print an argument about the early Church between Thomas Harding of Louvain and the apologist of the Church of England John Jewel, both parties erected a monument to the decay of dialogue. In the 1570s, after nearly two centuries of jibbing, it was concluded that if Catholic priests were to escape confusion in a country familiar with the vernacular scriptures, they had better not be left to translate the Vulgate in their heads, but provided with an official version of their own, the Bible of Reims and Douai. But those did best in the later sixteenth century whose humanist instincts or talents enabled them to treat the printed word not simply as a convenience but as an artistic opportunity, and though they were not only to be found among reformers (the Jesuit Edmund Campion is an obvious domestic example), the greatest among them was indisputably Calvin. His masterpiece, the *Institutes of Christian Religion*, first published by the young convert humanist in Basel in the year of Erasmus's death (1536), was finally issued from the press of Robert Estienne by the patriarch of Geneva five years before he himself died in 1564.

Calvin, as the classicist Scaliger said, wrote more elegantly than was decent for a theologian. He also gave a lot of thought to his work's formal structure, changing it with each edition; in both Latin and French its final shape had an artistic finality, a total graspability despite its massive size, which resulted from conscious experiment in a new medium. As he told his readers, he learnt as he wrote, and one of the things he learnt was that the order of matters proper to the lecture-room was not necessarily the right order in a work of art. By the end of Book III, when it finally appears, we have been waiting for predestination for a long time. So structured, the word acquired a new starkness and penetrative capacity. The *Institutes* did not replace the minister of the word, and was in practice as much a preacher's manual as a layman's companion; but it provided a common ground from which the preacher and his scripture-seeking congregation could proceed to higher things. It seems rather central to a modulation in Protestant experience, as Luther's conception of the word as audible and creative gave way to a feeling for the visible, portable, quotable text. I may be exaggerating this transition, but one substantive development in Reformation theology seems difficult to understand without it. As the Reformation became more typographical, so it became less sacramental. At the fateful conference held by the Landgrave Philip of Hesse at Marburg in 1529 Luther had spoken up for, and allegedly carved on the table, *Hoc est enim corpus meum* ('For this is my body'), as a voice of thunder, an oracular utterance of Christ. On the other side of the table Zwingli and Oecolampadius of Basel offered a scholarly and spiritually minded grammarian's interpretation of a text. As the century proceeded, it was generally their view which prevailed among the reformed, driving the symbolic traditionalists, in Germany, England and Sweden, to the margins of the field. With his conscious mind Calvin did his best to resist the tide, and to affirm that spiritual sacraments were not to be treated as things of straw; but his humanism worked against him, sabotaging his efforts at liturgical reconstruction and opening the sluices for the rhetoric of predestination. The tide had flooded his own communion by the time of the Synod of Dort (1618), and thereafter flooded a good deal of Catholic territory as well, before the perils of ink-divinity began to reveal themselves in the later seventeenth century.

It is widely held that, quite apart from its connection with humanist textualism, printing would have had a bad effect on liturgy anyway. This is not obvious. The press provided a vehicle for Thomas Cranmer's *Book of Common Prayer*, which at least in its first version of 1549 was a masterpiece (or collection of masterpieces) as unquestionable as Calvin's *Institutes*; a claim of the same order might be made for the Roman Ritual of 1612. But however splendid these achievements, they possessed a finality and uniformity which added something foreign to the genre, always inhibiting, often simply arresting, the invention and elaboration, the local and personal variety, which had been characteristic of the medieval liturgy. Where local rites managed to survive, they too were arrested: in France, the reducing of custom to print by sixteenth-century legal scholarship also entailed the printing of the multitude of local variations of the marriage rite. This helped to ensure their survival in face of Roman uniformity, but probably prevented any further incorporation of live social mores. It was certainly an ominous development.

In general the press was as much the enemy of the image as it was of ritual and symbol; but it was itself a manufacturer of images, and the sixteenth-century press was a great multiplier of those that could be regarded as adjuncts of the word. It was certainly a gift to martyrology, blotting out memories of the *Golden Legend* with the fierce actuality of the collections of Jean Crespin (*Livre des Martyrs*, 1554) and Foxe (*Acts and Monuments*, 1563), bursting off the page with eye-witness narratives, *ipsissima verba* of trials and last words, moments of heroism and brutality fixed for ever in woodcut and engraving. Deprived of other sustenance for the visual sense, Protestants feasted their eyes on these: if anything did, they converted present community into historical solidarity with past and future. The same resources were available to Catholics, and much used in the later sixteenth century in Rome, France, England and elsewhere. But it was fitting that, in the time and the place where they had their most powerful effect on the destinies of a nation—the rabid and exasperated Paris of the 1580s, convinced that the monarchy was selling it out to the Protestants—the images of Catholic martyrs were not to be found in books, but in huge tableaux expounded with markers to watching crowds. The redirection of solidarity effected by martyr-cults was surely as yet a marginal effect for Catholics, and I wonder if it occurred among Lutherans; it entered intimately into the consciousness of many other Protestants. Now they could *see* that the community of true Christians was a small body of witnesses to truth in continual struggle against the world and the powers of darkness. They would find themselves irresistibly drawn to the Apocalypse, or Book of Revelation, and to the Last Days when the slaughter of the martyrs would be avenged and Christ reign on earth with his saints. The Book of Revelation had not been the favourite reading of their founding fathers, who were right to fear the consequences of an obsession with it, but it was certainly predestined territory for the visual aid. It was as much as anything by putting a face to the Vision of St John that the press contributed to launching the experience of the gospel in another mode.

(iii) The Spirit

And it shall come to pass in the last days, saith God, I will pour out of my Spirit upon all flesh: and your sons and your daughters shall prophesy, and your young men shall see visions, and your old men shall dream dreams . . . and it shall come to pass, that whosoever shall call on the name of the Lord shall be saved.

(Acts 2: 17–21; Joel 2: 28–32)

Defenders of Catholicism said that the disintegration of the old regime would introduce the reign of millenarians, sectaries and minor prophets, and there were times when their anticipations of doom seemed to be turning out correct. The heritage of medieval dissent, though not in general very inspiring, was visible enough on the hilltops of Bohemia, and once the compensating super-

orthodoxy of the Germans had been shattered, might turn over-
night from a nightmare into a model. So in a small way it had done
for Luther, when at their public disputation at Leipzig in 1519 his
Catholic opponent John Eck persuaded him that he had been a
Hussite all the time. Except as a refuge, the Czechs proved a
broken reed, but the resources of German-speaking Catholicism
and German-speaking humanism proved unexpectedly fertile in
inspiring motives for dissent from Reformation orthodoxy.

It was the intellectuals who started it, when their restitution of a
textual Christianity got out of hand, as it did under the influence of
Andreas Carlstadt at Wittenberg, who did not like images, and of
Conrad Grebel at Zürich, who did not like music. Luther's return
from the Wartburg brought Carlstadt under control, but Zwingli
at Zürich had a tougher problem. His competitors were simply
arguing that what he had said about the Eucharist—that it was a
commemorative event which should follow as exactly as possible
the New Testament sources—ought self-evidently to be also true of
the other surviving sacrament, baptism. The New Testament data
were that the qualifications for baptism were repentance and belief
in Christ, its consequences the descent of the Holy Ghost, the
forgiveness of sins, and community of goods among the baptised.
Since infants had obviously not the qualifications they could
obviously not receive the benefits. With the heroic literalism which
marked their generation Zwingli's opponents therefore deduced
that neither they nor the rest of Christendom had been genuinely
baptised, and went off to baptise each other in the Rhine. They
also, on the same textual grounds, set out to preach the gospel to
every creature. In their disregard for actual Christian practice they
were quite likely not aware that in abolishing infant baptism they
had demolished the foundation-stone of Christian society; when
the point was brought home to them by the municipal authorities
in Zürich and elsewhere, they consulted their text and discovered
that the axe was laid to the root of the tree. It was time to separate
the wheat from the chaff, especially from the chaff of civil authority, with which Zwingli and others were inexcusably adulterat-
ing it. So was born, or reborn, the sectarianism of the gathered
Church.

There was never any chance that this mimetic radicalism would
get the vote of the average man: that it appealed to more than might
have been expected was due to its conflation with lively forces in

German Christianity with which official reformers failed sufficiently to reckon. One of these was the fraternal tradition, strongly
represented among reformed German cities in Strassburg, a city
whose fraternity structure resembled that of Venice. Its gardeners'
gild threw up in Clement Ziegler an indigenous prophet of something between traditional fraternity and Reformation sectarianism,
who failed to convert the peasants of the Black Forest but at home
offered an alternative model to the municipal reformation designed
by Martin Bucer. A city which also had a strong humanist
constituency and a thriving printing-press, Strassburg became for
some years around 1530 a haven for practically all the misfits,
intellectual and other, of the German-speaking Reformation; it was
a strong candidate for the role of New Jerusalem until it was beaten
to the tape by Münster in Westphalia and Bucer was able to
introduce reformed law and order.

Anabaptism progressed by drawing on a variety of powerful
motifs, some old, some new. The notion of absolute brotherhood,
in which all barriers would disappear and peace and love prevail,
was the most traditional. As I have said, it was endemic in
medieval Christianity, and during the 1470s had drawn crowds to
a prophet called the Drummer of Niclashausen in the territory of
the bishop of Würzburg, who had preached it under the patronage
of Our Lady. The idea was strengthened by being put more
exactly than it had hitherto been in the historical form of a revival
of primitive Christianity, the 'Restitution' which forms the theme
of G. H. Williams's book on the subject. From a practical point of
view there were two scriptural novelties which mattered more.
The calling to apostleship sent Anabaptists along the lifelines of
the Empire, in particular down the Rhine to the Netherlands and
the Hanseatic coasts, where they proved rather more welcome
than in the south. The severe persecution they received almost
everywhere heightened the millenarian anticipations expounded
by some of their prophets, and persuaded a lot of them to identify
themselves, as the Czech Taborites had done, with those passages
in the Book of Revelation that spoke of the vengeance to be meted
out to those who had slaughtered the saints.

All these motifs, plus iconoclasm, visions and undogmatic
fantasies about wealth, sex and power, were present in the regime
of Anabaptist immigrants from the Netherlands which ruled in
Münster from February 1534 to June the following year. The

fantasies dominated the totalitarian reign of Jan Bockelson of Leyden, a nine-month Carnival without a Lent. It seems reasonable enough for heirs of the Anabaptist tradition to protest that this theatrical producer, graduate of the literary and artistic milieu of the Dutch Renaissance, is not a fair representative of their inheritance. The northern brethren kept their heads down until the States-General of the Netherlands offered them toleration in 1578, and they succeeded in passing on an acceptable model of the gathered Church to England and America. More systematically persecuted, the southerners, many of whom came from the Tyrol, escaped down the Danube to practise godly communism quietly in Moravia.

Among a multitude of prophets and apostles, who were an irritation to more conventional reformers but not much more, German Christianity produced one indisputably major competitor, the Saxon Thomas Muentzer. What made Muentzer a major prophet, apart from a variety of remarkable talents, was that he was quite as penetrating a biblical theologian, and had as learned a grasp of Christian and classical tradition, as Luther or Calvin. His particular insight also struck a sensitive place in the Christianity of his time. Muentzer was a theologian of the Holy Ghost: his contribution was to point out to his colleagues, something they were nervous about recognising, that if they were going to let God be God they had, as well as liberating the fatherhood of the Father and the wordhood of the Son, also to let the Spirit be Spirit. The Germans, as Luther himself had revealed to the public, were especially blessed with doctors of the Spirit: let them listen to them.

In 1516, when the youngish Luther had published the vernacular compendium of fourteenth-century German mystical teaching, the *Theologia deutsch*, he was feeding another tributary into an extremely powerful current. Prophetic demands for an intenser cultivation of the Spirit, often cast in the historical mould of Abbot Joachim of Fiore's three ascending ages of the world (the age of the Father, the age of the Son, and the age of the Spirit), had been a commonplace of traditional Christianity. They throve upon its abhorrence of the flesh. But they had been, so to speak, a marginal commonplace, like God's *potestas absoluta* as conceived by nominalist theologians: something for emergencies. Of the various happenings which had by now shifted this commonplace into the centre, the advent of Erasmus and his spiritual anti-sacramentalism was the most obvious, even if he had complicated the theological issue by rejecting as spurious a rather crucial text about the equality of the Holy Ghost with the Father and the Son. Behind Erasmus stood Plato, culture-hero of the enemies of school-divinity, received directly by the Florentines and indirectly by almost everyone through St Augustine; Augustine's *On the Spirit and the Letter*, though mainly a discussion of justification by faith, was a text universally venerated. It was impossible for a man of any culture at all in the early sixteenth century to be hostile to a spiritual Christianity, though what exactly that was the opposite of was another question.

The trouble with the Spirit, from the point of view of organised Christianity, has always been that it bloweth (or, as Caspar Schwenckfeld phrased it, spiriteth) where it listeth. It had not done the German mystics much good in the fourteenth century, and did not now recommend a number of Italians, or Spaniards like Ignatius Loyola and Teresa of Ávila, to their respective inquisitions. As a kind of spirit of permanent revolution it was a difficult guest in any Church. For the orthodox reformers it raised the additional problem that they were committed to the scriptural word as the only reliable medium of communication between God and the Christian, and to the faith which came by hearing it.

What was for magisterial reformers a problem, was for Muentzer a revelation. Though he died young, had time to write little or nothing at leisure, and was generally execrated as a monster of sedition, it seems right to think of him as the master of Reformation dissent. With some exaggeration he can be said to have enunciated a doctrine which a lot of extremely independent minds —the Silesian gentleman Schwenckfeld, the cosmographer Sebastian Franck, the doctor Servetus, as well as Anabaptists strictly speaking—elaborated in their various ways. The doctrine contained three affirmations, which I shall now set down too crudely. The first was that the Spirit was superior to the Word, that God's direct speaking to the soul was a more certain witness of truth than the plain scriptural text: the letter killed but the spirit quickened. This meant that the scriptural words on the page were the outer covering of an inner word which had to be discerned. It also meant that God, who was not, in Muentzer's favourite phrase, a dumb God, had other ways of communicating with mankind, as by the continuing inspiration of his prophets, by visions, and by the witness of all creation. In Muentzer's amazing sermon to the Saxon princes on the second chapter of the Book of Daniel the burden of this teaching was to identify the official reformers, almost before they had got started, as letter-mongering scribes, and to assert the independent access of the 'common man', including the illiterate man, to the spirit of Christ.

Since the spirit was at odds with the flesh, the incarnation of Christ would need reinterpretation. Servetus was burned by Calvin for revising the Trinity, and communities which formally rejected the doctrine were founded by Italian *émigrés* in the multidenominational commonwealth of Poland. Theirs was a problem which preoccupied practically all the spiritual reformers, with the exception of Muentzer himself, in whom the instincts and iconography of late medieval Christendom seem to have been too strongly embedded. For many, the solution was to deny that the flesh which Christ had taken was an actual biological flesh received from his mother. It was, they held, a 'celestial flesh' or uncreated substance, eternally pre-existent, to which the phenomenal appearances of the man Christ served as a sort of Platonic shadow. Considering what has been said on the subject here, it is nice to find G. H. Williams concluding that the source of their problem was a nervous twitch about Anselm's doctrine of the Redemption, and a confused anxiety to replace it by something else. It was also, positively in this case, related to the pre-Reformation devotional tradition about the Eucharist, and in particular to those cases where intense feelings about spiritual communion with Christ had relegated the actual consumption of the Host to a minor role. Supported by a famous passage from St John about the spirit and the flesh, the feeling had spilled over into the spiritual 'sacramentarianism' represented by the Zwinglian party at the Marburg conference, and guided Calvin's attempt to construct a reformed eucharistic doctrine which everyone could accept. Among the dissenters it is best represented by the characteristic doctrine of Schwenckfeld that in the present state of Christendom the physical administration of the Eucharist ought to be suspended until further notice.

By reading 'nature' or 'natural kinship' for 'flesh', and keeping steadily in view the datum that Christ's baptism was a regeneration in the Holy Spirit, one readily arrived at strictly Anabaptist conclusions. Muentzer himself did not consistently do so, for a reason which accounts for his greater resemblance to the millenarians of Münster than to the mainstream of Anabaptism. It also accounts for his identification with the cause of the embattled German peasants of 1524–5, which brought about his death. Believers' baptism was a doctrine of division, and not just in the eyes of princely bureaucrats and unity-haunted municipalities; it provoked a growl from the average soul in defence of his conviction that through their baptism he and his children were living in Christianity. Anabaptists sharpened the sectarian edge of militant fraternity, millenarian hope, and the aping of the primitive Church on an anthology of texts about the swordlike character of spiritual discernment. But where they mainly concentrated on separating the wheat from the chaff, Muentzer found his mission in putting the axe to the tree of carnal authority. Because the sources of his inspiration were different, his message was framed in the language of unity, not of separation. What the old German doctors had told him was that the defining characteristic of the Spirit was oneness, that twoness was the opposite of oneness, and that holiness entailed not separation but the swallowing of the parts by the whole. Such nuances, it is true, were not very obvious to outsiders, and least of all to the common man in whose name Muentzer claimed to be speaking. Even to an intelligentsia inclined to sympathise with both these aspirations, the fruits of the Spirit appeared to be simply babel and confusion. Felt from within, in Münster possibly and Moravia certainly, in the pastures of Frisia or the forests of Essex, they were the communion of saints, the unity of the Spirit in the bond of peace.

By what means these doctrines were transmitted to the England of the Interregnum, more than a century later, and whether indeed an actual transmission was called for, are difficult questions. Perhaps we should think of them as spores secreted in a Christian culture, guaranteed to produce mushrooms at a certain temperature. In any case, no one who turns from the history of radical Christianity in the Germany of the 1520s and 1530s to the England of the 1640s and 1650s can fail to get the feeling that he has been there before. There were of course differences: the collapsed establishment was not the traditional Church but a reformed Church of England with eighty years of life behind it; the learned model for reconstructing it was not Luther's Wittenberg or Zwingli's Zürich but, more or less, Calvin's Geneva. One of the passions liberated was a rather particular creation of English Protestant history. Somehow, the operations of the word of God as preached by the ministers of the reformed Church of England had nurtured in many of their hearers another vision of the gathered Church; its characteristics have been defined as separation from the world, covenanted fellowship, freedom of choice and visible holiness. Exactly how, is something of a mystery, and so is exactly when. From within, the vision has been seen as endemic in English Protestantism from the start, as the effect of a domesticating or privatising tendency in English Calvinist evangelism after 1600, and as a reaction to the shock of a bench of reactionary bishops in the 1630s, to the discovery in the 1640s that the monarch was a limb of Antichrist and the end of the world at hand, or to the influence of *émigrés* returning from Holland or New England. From outside, its origins have been discerned in the structure of industrious households, in lay supremacy or military organisation.

Powerful as it was at the time and, as the mainspring of English nonconformity, influential later in the formation of a particularly English religious universe, the tradition of the gathered Church, or congregationalism, did not usually promote radical changes in the exterior world. It remained Calvinist in its language and ethos, and even where it adopted adult baptism rarely drew the social conclusions which Anabaptists had drawn. Despite its theory it proved capable of integration into established Churches, as briefly by Cromwell and more permanently in New England. It did not prove able to contain, and in spite of itself clearly encouraged, the extraordinary multiplication of English religious expressions which characterised the Interregnum. By 1650 it had been put on the defensive, not by the competition from orthodox Presbyterianism which it had succeeded in beating off, but by a haemorrhage of members dismayed by the quarrels of Protestants and seeking for something more fulfilling or more unifying than the word as mediated by Calvin; whence they were known as 'seekers'.

Some found the answer in the active millenarianism of the Fifth Monarchists, who interpreted the prophecy of Daniel rather differently from Muentzer, but like him held that in these latter days it was not sufficient for the saints to gather apart from the contagion of the world; they must take the material sword in hand, demolish all existing government and bring about a theocratic regime of godly discipline where Christ at his coming again would find a home. A body of terrorists, attractive to military men, they did not depart very much from the mainstream of English Reformation doctrine, had influence within the Commonwealth establishment, and when they were deceived in their hope that Cromwell was their man went in for *coups d'état*, fortunately unsuccessful.

These were a small and dedicated band; most seekers found what they were looking for by turning from the word to some version of Muentzer's doctrine of the Spirit. Not that one can make a drastic distinction between spiritualists and millenarians, since the pouring forth of the Spirit was one of the authorised signs of the latter days. The ground had been prepared by some limited importation of Anabaptist beliefs across the North Sea, and by some thriving strains in English godliness: the prophetic strain, the devotional strain which insisted on the primacy of private religious experience, and the inspirational view of prayer, of liturgy and (in the sects) of the qualifications for ministry. There had been a tension between the predestinarian ministry and a godly constituency partial to free will and spiritual perfection; we can regard the explosion of spiritual Christianity as a victory of the hearers, often of the female hearers, over the preachers of the word.

Through what sounds at first hearing a frightful cacophony the themes of German radicalism and its medieval precursors could now be heard, repeated in the variety of individual voices: the voice of the Ranters, who believed that the elect could not sin; the voice of Gerrard Winstanley, who tried to bring oneness down to earth by digging up St George's Hill in the parish of Walton-on-Thames; the voice of George Fox and the Quakers, preachers of the inner light, who proved the movement's one permanent addition to English life and in the end absorbed many of the others, including Winstanley himself. All of them believed in the superiority of the immediate experience of the Spirit; all of them had visions, and maintained that prophecy was still alive. The Ranter Abiezer Coppe claimed that the vehicle of letter-observance which chiefly needed to be overcome was the Ten Commandments, and also identified himself with God: which was less unwonted as a spiritual doctrine than in the bizarrely literal expression which he gave it. Fox, preaching to confused sectarians in the north the spirit of Jesus as a withdrawal from exterior 'notions' and 'professions', extolled (not before time) the virtue of silence among the friends of

God, and offered to all men a version of what the Middle Ages would have called the negative way to sanctification. Winstanley called for the Spirit to rule over the flesh, and liked to identify it with what he called Reason, meaning something like transcendental equity indwelling in the consciences or altruism of men. Technically the Ranters seem to have been predestinarians, the rest were evidently believers in free will; but it seems inappropriately literal to take such distinctions too seriously. Samuel Fisher, who passed from Ranting to Quakerism, took up (a little before French Catholics mounted a formidable attack from the same direction) the textual criticism of the Bible as a weapon against 'teachers and Text-men'.

Though none of them exactly held the German doctrine of Christ's celestial flesh, none of them believed either, exactly, that Christians owed their salvation to an atonement made for human sin by a historical Jesus. Without exception they saw the Christ who mattered as a presence diffused through the persons of the saints, an abstract entity whose distinction from the Holy Spirit had collapsed. Winstanley, who expressed this belief strongly, though not more strongly than Ranters and Quakers, has therefore been held not to have believed in a transcendental God at all, which seems untrue.

Finally they all believed, like Muentzer, that the Spirit was one, and perfect oneness the mark of communities in which the Spirit ruled; under the Spirit, to borrow a phrase from the Ranter Coppe, men would be confounded into universality. The Quakers took this as an injunction to ignore worldly hierarchy and use the fraternal 'thou' in speaking to all men. Winstanley saw the rule of the Spirit over the flesh as entailing the abolition of property and wage-labour. The Ranters, who signified their own victory over the flesh by calling themselves God's *one* flesh, witnessed against both hierarchy and property, adding monogamous marriage and the separate family to the obstacles to true community.

Though absorbing to contemplate, the adventures of the spiritual radicals were in the end only a footnote to the history of the transformations of Christendom. This was not chiefly because their social doctrines antagonised the authorities, since they rather throve on persecution. It was more because their millenarian background inhibited them from preaching the sort of mysticism of everyday life which would accommodate the conventional wisdom that good fences make good neighbours. It seems too strong to say that they were the end of an old song, not the beginning of a new one, for they were all scripturalists in their fashion and their feelings about oneness corresponded to something general in the Reformation; the Quakers are after all still with us. But on the whole they strike one as a bit old-fashioned, inhabitants of a moral universe shaped by the deadly sins. To the lack of staying-power characteristic of extraordinary motions of the Spirit they added the anachronism of having been born into a civilisation of the word: in the long run, moreover, a civilisation of the printed word. One answer to the Anabaptists was the baptismal register; another was the catechism. The spirituals could not compete in this field: imagine a Ranter catechism. In early modern Europe, more than is probably always the case, the age of the Spirit was either gone, or not yet come.

7 The Institution of Christian Religion

Little as humanists and reformers might find to commend in the traditional practice of the sacraments, there was no arguing with the doctrine of Augustine and the old Church that sacraments were the skeleton of the social body. If you wished the Church to remain a social body, you had better have sacraments; what was decided about sacraments would determine what sort of social body the new Church was to be. The point was driven home to all reformers by their rude confrontation with the spiritual radicals. In the light of this disagreeable experience it dawned upon them that all kinds of things by which they set great store—the Christian instruction of children, the integrity of the Christian household, the identity of the Church and the civil community—hung upon the traditional practice of infant baptism. They hastened to reaffirm it, along with the Eucharist, as one of the two symbolic acts whose performance had been commanded by Christ in the gospel.

Thus two sacraments replaced the seven of the old Church, and the three which Luther, keeping penance, had originally envisaged. In so far as the sacraments had provided a social system for the Christian laity, Luther's scheme, except that he excluded marriage, was only a version of the traditional one. This consisted in effect of only four of the mystic seven, since ordination, extreme unction and confirmation can be excluded, and the rest formed a tripartite structure: the rites of kinship (baptism and marriage) led through the rite of reconciliation (penance) to the rite of unity (the Eucharist). Whatever may in general have been the ground for the trinitarianism deeply ingrained in medieval minds, here it meant a belief that between the alpha and the omega of Christian society lay a region of dubious conflict which called for its own ritual provision. In settling for two sacraments alone the reformers implied the humanists' conviction that this area could be dealt with by other means, by instruction, counsel, exhortation or legislation; and though it retained the intermediary sacrament, the Catholic

Church proceeded on somewhat the same assumptions. Explicitly in one case, implicitly in the other, they were leaving out the second act from the ritual, and hence the social performance.

(i) The Fourth Commandment

The Reformation brought to a conclusion the process of replacing the seven deadly sins by the Ten Commandments as the system of Christian ethics; the first of them to deal with the Christian's duties to his neighbour rather than to God was 'Honour thy father and thy mother'. What counted for himself and for Catholics as the fourth commandment, and as the fifth for Calvin and others who elevated the prohibition of graven images to independent status, was, said Luther, the foundation stone of all social and political obligation among Christians. It was also an injunction to be taken in its literal sense. Nobody, it is true, supposed the commandment to mean no more than it literally said: paternity would always be held to inhere in the authorities of Church and State, and reformers as well as Catholics would expound the commandment as requiring obedience to them. But whereas for Catholics metaphorical meanings were the essential burden of the commandment, for reformers actual parenthood became the crux; the claim of the civil authority to obedience might be construed as a residual authority to act *in loco parentis* where for one reason or another the actual parent was incompetent to fulfil his or her role. But since in Lutheran practice this turned out to be the usual case, the immediate beneficiary of an insistence on fatherhood was the metaphorical prince rather than the literal father. Nobody seems to have taken much notice that the commandment put mothers on a level with fathers. Reformers had the excuse that, what with Mother Church and Our Lady, Christians had had rather a lot of mothering already; but the failure to read past the first three words of the commandment was more general than this, and it seems simplest to put it down to the chauvinism of a male constituency.

This elevation of a literal paternity was bound to make a difference to the practice of the sacrament of baptism. Hostility to Anabaptists, and a general conviction that ritual kinship was a myth, also indicated the natural parents as the parties into whose hands the baptised infant should be delivered. But the tradition of baptismal exogenesis remained strong, both in theology and in popular feeling, and the more traditional reformers were sensitive to the reflection that abolishing godparenthood would be a sad blow to Christian sociability. Luther himself went no further than to reject spiritual relationship as a bar to marriage: he made as much of the opportunity of godparenthood presented by his withdrawal from the religious life as he did of the chance of fatherhood; godparents retained their historic role in his baptismal rite. It has been suggested that in Lutheran practice there was a tendency for the pastor's wife to act as universal godmother, which might have been quite an effective way of conveying the implications of the fourth commandment to the masses.[13] Calvin found the contrast more of a problem, since he had learnt from Zwingli and Bucer to defend infant baptism by applying to Christians the Old Testament idea of a covenant between God and a historic people, Abraham and his seed. He seems to have kept silence about godparents, leaving them out of his ritual but regarding them perhaps as one of his 'tolerable absurdities'; French Calvinists, oddly at one with Rome, seem to have adopted a single male godparent. But the obvious drift of his teaching was to reverse the historic exclusion of natural parents, and his English followers were surely correct in so interpreting him. Faced with Thomas Cranmer's traditionalist regime, which was much the same as Luther's, they struggled to enforce the discipline that only the natural parents might present and receive their children at baptism, and that an alternative parenthood was no more than something to fall back on if these were lacking. Their view prevailed in the Westminster Assembly of 1643–53, and thus became for a time the discipline of the English Church; it was upset at the Restoration.

The enhancement of the role of natural parents in the formal baptism was somewhat qualified by the rules that it should be performed in public at service-time, and that women were not fit ministers of it. Nevertheless, the idea of the covenant was widely influential outside the Presbyterian tradition, and not only in New England, where it was a burning question. Besides answering the Anabaptists, it best represented the conviction prevailing among the educated that initiation into Christianity was not really achieved by symbolic rituals but by instructing children in their faith. Godparenthood was ill designed to do this, and the more instruction figured on the menu of Christianity the less meaningful an institution it appeared. Even those reformed communities which retained it did not, with one or two exceptions among conservative Elizabethan parsons, think it worth recording in their baptismal registers; if the seventeenth-century Essex parson Ralph Josselin was anything to go by, the English clergy thought it a tolerable folk-custom of little significance. The Catholic Church did indeed continue to require godparents to be recorded, but what had been in the sixteenth century its principal motive for registration—to prevent the marriage of people joined by spiritual relationship—had become by the eighteenth the small print in a register of natural parents and their children. For the Catholic population a creation of ritual friendship continued to be the principal social significance of baptism; but this was not encouraged by the Counter-Reformation clergy, rather the reverse. The Council of Trent made one last effort to relaunch the single Roman godfather, but finally fell back on a pair of symbolic parents, one of either sex. This may seem a piece of superfluous mimicry: where the medieval English rite had laid on the godmother the obligation of teaching the child its prayers, the Roman Ritual of 1612 required the priest to remind the natural parents of their duty of Christian instruction. It must have assumed that they would be present at the baptism, which was not traditional practice.

In reality the consensus of Protestant and Catholic reformations converged, not upon the instructional role of parents, but on the catechising duties of the clergy. The mutation of the word 'catechism', from meaning an exorcism performed before baptism to meaning a course of instruction supervening a good while after it, did not in fact entail any significant redistribution of authority from clergy to laity. The ink was scarcely dry on Luther's *Shorter Catechism* (1529), framed as a dialogue between father and child, when evangelical authorities had thrown up the sponge and passed the responsibility to the clergy; this became the rule in Lutheran churches. The Genevan tradition, launched by Calvin's ill-conceived *Formulaire d'instruire les enfants en la Chrétienté* of 1541 and the more viable *Heidelberg Catechism* of 1563, may have tried to keep the balance for longer; but most of the evidence comes from England, where Calvinists were often unhappy with the doctrine being taught by the parish clergy. Among both Catholics and Protestants domestic catechising only really occurred where they were condemned to privacy by a hostile or unsympathetic establishment. Hence the Church of England hierarchy was not out of step with the general practice of reformed Churches in taking it for granted that catechism was a parochial activity, and that parishes would be well edified if their children spent Sunday afternoons learning by rote the obligations which had been undertaken for them at their baptism. There was also no obstacle, in the state of alarm inspired by the success of Reformation catechising, to Catholic borrowing of the outlines of Reformation catechisms as a guide to their own efforts in the field, as the Jesuits did on a large scale: Peter Canisius from Luther in Germany (1556), Émond Auger from Calvin in France (1563). In Italy Robert Bellarmine worked, rather later, on lines of his own derived from the *Catechism of the Council of Trent*. By about 1600 there can have been few languages in which a catechism was not available, more or less well designed for children to learn by heart. Although the general tendency was towards standardisation, seventeenth-century France seems almost as rich in examples as sixteenth-century Germany, since the Gallican tradition of episcopal independence encouraged bishops to compose their own. As in reformed Churches the chief agent of catechism was the parish priest. He was assisted in Italy by 'schools' (or fraternities) of Christian doctrine which began to spring up in Lombardy in the mid-century, were promoted both by the Counter-Reformation episcopate in the north and by the pope in Rome, and seem to have included both priests and laymen; they apparently worked without a set text until Bellarmine provided one. Bellarmine's catechism was indeed advertised as suitable for parents and masters of households as well as for priests or professional catechists; but the general view of the Counter-Reformation clergy was that it was hard enough to get parents to send their children along to catechism, never mind doing it themselves. I doubt if the experience of reformed Churches was much different.

The carrying to the masses of these pedagogical versions of Christianity probably had in the long run more considerable effects than any other innovation of the sixteenth century. Though catechism was in form an oral mode of instruction, it is a case where the possibility of typographical tyranny does need to be considered. A great deal of talent and imagination certainly went into it, provided in the first place by Luther and a multitude of emulators in Lutheran countries during the decades after 1530, and later by the Jesuits, who were not afraid of appearing childish, took account of symbols and visual aids, and on the whole respected the limits of memory. Bellarmine left out the eight beatitudes on the grounds that nobody could remember more than seven of anything. The French made use of a tradition of vernacular versification already developed in the fifteenth century. Catechism cleared the ground for systems of primary education in the countryside, an effect becoming visible in France before 1700.

Against that one must set its effect in reducing Christianity to whatever could be taught and learnt. It taught prayers, as parents, godmothers or priests had done before the Reformation, but spent more time explaining what the words meant. It expounded the Creed and the Ten Commandments, which were both easier and more congenial to explain than the seven deadly sins; for Catholics the Creed came first, for Lutherans the Commandments, rather on the principle of getting the worst over first. It added for children of the reformed a good deal of instruction about behaviour and deference to parents and civil authorities, and for those of Catholics another set of commandments concerning religious observance; these had been newly extracted from the confessional summae of the fifteenth century and were described as the commandments of the Church. Catechism was well designed to instil obedience and mark out boundaries, between versions of the Reformation as much as between Protestants and Catholics, and it could be the foundation of a reflective Christian life. It was less well adapted to inspiring a sense of the Church as a *communitas*, a feeling for the sacraments as social institutions, or simply the love of one's neighbour.

For Catholics, perhaps for everybody, one consequence of catechism was the surrender of large areas of everyday social practice to the prophets of civility, whose injunctions were commonly dinned into children alongside the Creed and the Commandments. Erasmus, who would not have been much gratified by the catechisms themselves, could here have his revenge, since the basic text on civil mores was his apparently modest work on improving the manners of children. Unlike other aspects of Erasmus's legacy, this maintained an unbroken and increasing influence until its triumph in the eighteenth century. It was elaborated in the papal diplomat Giovanni della Casa's *Galatea* (1558), which Jesuits used as a textbook of behaviour, and by a regiment of French authors on 'Christian civility' culminating in Jean-Baptiste de la Salle, whose *Règles de la bienséance et de la civilité chrétienne*, published in 1713, carried all before it for a century. By de la Salle's time the trinity of catechism, civility and literacy was universally acknowledged in the West as the constellation which should govern the education of children. Differences between versions of Christianity were probably no longer significant, and the limitation by rank of the teaching of civility was being broken down. It dealt with table-manners, bodily deportment, the touchable, the mentionable and the noticeable, and as in the case of catechism its chief agent was not the household but the school. It is difficult to know from what sort of date it was being spontaneously promoted by parents. Despite the celebrated counter-example of the ramshackle upbringing of King Louis XIII of France, the early to middle seventeenth century seems a reasonable guess for gentry and bourgeoisie; for the rest of the population Erasmian table-manners can hardly have pre-dated the cheap fork, held up by technical difficulties which only seem to have been solved by the industrial revolution.[14]

To see the coming of the fork as an event in the history of Christianity, we could do worse than pay attention to the views of the Venetian inquisitors who in 1573 commented unfavourably on a large painting by Paolo Veronese intended to represent the Last Supper. They held that it was not an admissible portrayal of the event on the grounds, among others, that it showed an apostle preparing to eat his supper with a fork. (Veronese made things worse by claiming that it was not a fork but a toothpick, and the painting ended up as the *Feast in the House of Levi*.) In a Christianity to which the rites of commensality meant a good deal, a system of table-manners which interdicted direct access to a single dish or cup could be a momentous innovation. Nothing, least of all the memorial reconstruction of sacramentarians, could convert the Lord's Supper into an exercise in civility: as civility conquered the table, the rites of domestic commensality and the rites of Christianity went their different ways. Fish-eating certainly survived longer than Erasmus, who wrote a comic dialogue against it, would have wished. It was supported, at least in England, by the anxiety of governments that their navies would collapse if it were given up; by the intensified loyalty of Catholics to a practice which came to distinguish them from others; and by some resistance on the part of housewives to the abolition of their single priestly function. But fasting and abstinence were always hard to reconcile with civility, and where they continued were a good deal transformed by the decline of the common dish. Or so one may gather from the recommendation to eighteenth-century Catholics to exercise self-denial at meals by passing over some particularly tasty morsel, but to take care not to be seen doing so. Grace before and after meals was encouraged by catechisms both Catholic and reformed, and had the effect, of which Thomas Cranmer would have approved, of turning the domestic meal into a sacrifice of praise and thanksgiving.

The observation of the fourth commandment entailed a previous deference to the scriptural injunction to increase and multiply; it would be strange if the revaluation of natural paternity (and theoretically of natural maternity as well) had not done something to alter the profile of sexuality in the consciousness of Christians. In itself the persuasion that conjugal procreation was the only legitimate outlet for sexual acts was no stronger among Reformation theologians than among those of the medieval Church. The Reformation probably did something to reinforce it by helping to ensure the primacy in this field of the views of theologians over those of canon lawyers, by instituting the marriage of the clergy, by looking rather harder at male adultery, and by closing brothels. But in the state of opinion which inspired the marriage decree of the Council of Trent, the main deduction from the commandment was that the marriage choices of children ought to be more strictly governed by their parents; this may have had the effect, paradoxical and certainly contrary to Luther's intention, of somewhat delaying their access to marriage and sexual relations. There may possibly have been a general tendency for the age of marriage to rise between 1400 and 1700, and Pierre Chaunu (*Le Temps des réformes,* 1975) has given the impression of believing that the transformation of Christianity is somehow to be explained as an attempt to deal with the consequences of it. The demographer's computer may eventually have something interesting to say about the early modern history of sexuality among the unmarried young; as a guide to the history of married couples it has a knack of putting the cart before the horse. Apart from the revaluation of the fourth commandment, there were other developments in Christianity tending to delay the sexual experience of the young. One of them was the campaign to restrict the sharing of beds to married couples, which was in the long run to revolutionise the layout of houses; it had had some effect, at least among the upper classes, by 1700. This must have made entrance into the marriage bed, particularly when the social rites accompanying the event were frowned upon, more of a leap in the dark than hitherto. The most plausible deduction from the demographic figures is that there was some increase in the age at marriage of women: in the course of the seventeenth century it looks as if it became more normal than before for the age of a wife to correspond roughly to that of her husband, though this was actually opposed by Reformation critics as dangerous to godly patriarchy.

Such changes, if they occurred, would help to account for the quantity of advice to married couples which was a feature of Christian writing after the Reformation, and for the tone of domestic romanticism which has been claimed as a peculiar contribution of English Protestant authors. There may be something in the claim, though it made little difference to their recommendations about actual conduct. The quantity of writing seems to signify an intention to give conjugal society a higher place among the manifestations of Christian love than it had normally received before the Reformation. It is possible that Protestant writers, though less inclined to get down to sexual brass tacks than Catholic ones, proved in the long run more capable of getting sexual satisfactions a benevolent hearing under this head. Both inherited the Augustinian tradition, systematised in the pre-Reformation confessional manuals, that sexual relations between the married, if not directed intentionally towards childbearing, were always venially sinful, and if engaged in merely for the pleasure of it, mortally so.

If Jeremy Taylor's devotional classic *Holy Living* was anything to go by, English Protestant couples were being advised by 1650 that they might legitimately indulge to cheer themselves up or express fondness. During the previous century or so, a fairly vigorous effort had been made among Catholics to turn the subject round; but it had not in the end succeeded. Thirty years before the Reformation the Augustinian consensus had been shaken by the Paris theologian Martin le Maistre, who held that mutual comfort entitled couples to any amount of reasonably orthodox sexual gratification. The view was generally followed by the Thomists of the early sixteenth century and later became in the hands of the Jesuit Tomas Sánchez the foundation of a highly developed treatment of sexuality in conjugal society (*De sancto matrimonii sacramento*, 1602–5). Sánchez, however, provoked a puritan reaction which by the 1640s had taken shape in the Jansenist tradition of Antoine Arnauld and Pascal, and in this case found an ally in the arithmetic favoured in Rome. After Trent, couples were advised of their duty to breed more Catholics with an insistence which left little or no room for refinements of conjugal gratification. In practice it is probably true that in the course of the seventeenth century the tone of married life was in general becoming more affectionate, or at least more intense, among couples of all denominations: this has been deduced from the attitude to each other shown by French Catholic couples in their wills. But Catholicism, at least, does not seem to have managed to give the fact much in the way of theological support; it was perhaps a hindrance that Erasmus had not cared to extend his concept of civility to conjugal relations.

The fifteenth century had had two competing conceptions of the Holy Family, one larger and one smaller; after the middle of the seventeenth, magisterial Christianity of whatever complexion had only one. God's ordinance for Christians was the domestic *familia*, which consisted of a couple united by nature and by Pauline bonds of affection and respect; of children born and brought up (with the help of the clergy and schoolmasters) to fear the Lord, honour their parents, learn their letters, know their faith, and wipe their noses; and preferably of servants in the status of artificial children. It was as much an ideal construct as the tentacular chain of affectionate relations cultivated by tradition; but as an ideal it acquired an unquestionable authority sufficient to drive competing conceptions, which might in the abstract have as good or better a claim to be Christian, towards the undergrowth of folklore or the marginality of the sects. The authority was not, needless to say, solely that of a commandment of God; or at least the commandment had various auxiliaries. One was that of the classical, and particularly the Roman, world. The model of the Roman *familia* was a powerful presence from the fifteenth-century Italian humanists onwards, and well before the Reformation it had coalesced with the ambitions of some Italian governments to encourage a familial privacy which, it has been argued, cleared the public scene of family alliances, parties, and other obstacles to the advance of political authoritarianism. Shorter on the classics but stronger on the Commandments, Lutheran Germany probably underwent a similar process. The intensity of French traditionalism proved a formidable obstruction, and here the forces of Christian domesticity met in more or less self-conscious opposition the forces of Christian alliance. From reformed Geneva the French had been told that Old Testament precepts about brotherhood, for instance in the prohibition of usury, were anthropological survivals, while those about fatherhood were essential to Christian sanctification. From Catholic Lyon, after a brief Protestant regime which had driven streets through graveyards and trodden on the toes of fraternities, the Jesuit Émond Auger and the Franciscan Jean Benedicti (*La Somme des péchez,* 1584) replied by restating, with a vigour worthy of Thomas More, St Augustine's doctrine of the diffusion of charity by alliance and social rituals. They evoked a passionate response in the corporatism of the Catholic League, which stood up for compulsory fraternity against Protestants and the Crown, until its desertion by enlightened or terrified Catholics secured from the reign of Henri IV onwards an era of domesticated Christianities and unimpeded monarchy. In the British Isles the Irish Confederation of Kilkenny of 1641 was a manifestation similar in kind. Meanwhile the Church of England appears to have been undergoing a more muted version of the French conflict, between Calvinist promoters of godly domesticity and Arminian defenders of social friendship like the poet George Herbert.

There are limits, all the same, to the plausibility of reading the wars of religion as a battle between fatherhood and brotherhood. For one thing, it makes too little of axioms common to all sides; for another, Christian domesticity was sometimes more evidently an exterior consequence of the wars than an issue disputed in them. It was almost a necessary mode of existence of minority or dissenting communities, whatever their grounds for nonconformity or ultimate conception of the Church. Hence what may seem its peculiar precocity in England and the Dutch Republic was a tribute not only to the social theology of the Reformation, but also to the plurality of religious choices among the English and the Dutch. That apostle of the seventeenth-century domestic interior, Jan Vermeer of Delft, seems to have been a Catholic of sorts.

(ii) Discipline

Even Luther, who sometimes had visions of reviving the domestic Eucharist, never thought that the household was a convenient forum for penance, or the parental rod a suitable instrument for the reconciliation of sinners. True, Lutheran political theology did rather give the impression that sin could be taken care of by the patriarchal correction of the prince and his officers, but that was not entirely Luther's fault. In doing away with fasting and abstinence reformers had deprived the Christian household of the penitential function which it had hitherto fulfilled. But they would not have thought this a loss worth speaking of, since in eradicating the error of satisfaction for sin they were conscious of exploiting a general consensus of the learned. Civility, represented by Erasmus in his *Dialogue on Fish-eating*, supported them; scholastic theologians like Cajetan gave them the best of the argument by affirming that a Christian satisfaction must be 'medicinal', not 'vindictive'. Calvin found medicinality an acceptable notion, and More seems a lonely figure in his attempt to stand up against Tyndale for compensatory 'pain'. Thus the common sense of the learned, as often rather in the teeth of the common sense of the ignorant, came aboard the good ship *Metanoia*, propagating willy-nilly the Erasmian view that the only person who could harm a Christian was himself, and that deliverance from sin lay not in some objective restitution of exterior relations, but in changing the self.

The word for this enterprise, once its traditional application to penitential whipping had been discarded, was *disciplina*, and the difference between it and penance was that, while penance was something you did, discipline was something you learnt. Followers of Calvin had a habit of claiming it as their own invention, but the word was widely used by others, including the Council of Trent and its successor bishops. In principle, it simply meant the opposite of doctrine, the province of the learner; in ecclesiastical usage it meant whatever in Christianity had to do with behaviour as against belief, and the means which might be adopted for ensuring the diffusion of Christian behaviour. In practice it came to cover the range of matters which had hitherto been dealt with by penance. Reformers from all points of the compass were agreed that historic penance would not do, that the version of it practised by ecclesiastical courts was no way of inculcating Christian behaviour, and that prevention was better than cure. The most enterprising of them envisaged two radically different ways of supplying the deficiency, both of which may, by doing some violence to sixteenth-century terminology, be described as discipline.

In Catholicism the solution, which relied very much on developments in the practice of confession propagated during the fifteenth century, was to use the obligation to resort to the sacrament of penance as an incentive for the systematic interior monitoring by the individual of his own life. No more than an aspect of the interior dialogue preached in the *Imitation of Christ*, the examination of conscience became the subject of a plethora of fifteenth-century technical treatises which resembled the exercises in the art of memory investigated by Frances Yates; they were synthesised in unwieldy form by one of Erasmus's bugbears, the Sorbonnist Jan Mombaer. Cumbersome as it was, this corpus bore witness to a desire to shift the emphasis in sacramental penance from satisfaction following confession to interior discipline preceding it. It fell in readily with the Dominican view of the medicinal functions of the sacrament, and at the beginning of the sixteenth century was being propagated by them with a vigour which moved Luther to protest.

When the issue between the Dominicans and Luther over indulgences had clarified itself, what was left was a radical disagreement about the merits or possibility of systematic and exhaustive examination of conscience as an adjunct to confession. Luther's attack on the practice provided the principal grounds for his condemnation in 1520, and continued to be remembered against him through the Council of Trent and after; originally something of a school-point as between two theological schools and 'religious' traditions, the dispute turned out to have grave consequences in creating Catholic and Protestant ways of life incommunicable to each other. Taken up in the more strenuous, more outward- and forward-looking version of the interior conversation sketched by Ignatius Loyola in his *Spiritual Exercises* as both a companion for daily living and a guide through crises of individual conversion, the examination of conscience grew into a general programme of devout self-consciousness and a model of the Christian life characteristic of post-Reformation Catholicism. It proved capable, in the hands of later Jesuits, or of others like the Savoyard bishop and spiritual counsellor François de Sales, of adaptation to varieties of personal complexion and talent, of vocation, sex and social position. After a century or so it had begun to transform the practice of communion as well as that of confession, and was becoming an obligatory part of individual prayer for Catholics who prayed. It had launched the new profession of director of conscience and the new science of casuistry; it had inspired missionaries and female activists, had helped to interiorise the image and concentrate the minds of metaphysical poets. By mapping a rich territory on which the early reformers had turned their back, it had done an enormous amount for the reinvigoration of Catholicism. Like justification by faith it had drawbacks, some of which explain the ill feeling between Jesuits and Jansenists in seventeenth-century France. Among the devout it had done for the sacramental solidarity of traditional Catholicism; it had transcended the barrier between laymen and priests, or at least religious, at the expense of erecting a new one between the minority of the laity who practised it and the majority who did not. By linking the devout or the merely well-off more closely with their spiritual guides than with the rest of the population, it had bred the pious faction illustrated by Pascal's *Provincial Letters*. It probably helped to edge the masses from the sacramental to the superstitious.

Much the same fate befell the reformers, who were in the mean time attempting to supply the place of penance by the practice of exterior discipline. Among their founding fathers the proponent of *disciplina* was the guide of the Strassburg reformation, the former Dominican Martin Bucer. Alarmed by the social disintegration which seemed to be the immediate consequence of the liberation of the word, Bucer had preached the necessity of instituting a scriptural government of exterior behaviour with an insistence which his hearers, in Germany and in England (where he retired in 1549 under pressure from Charles V, and died two years later), sometimes found tiresome. Calvin, who was in this respect his pupil, gave the idea the particular form of moral supervision by ministry and congregational elders which was what most Protestants understood by discipline thereafter.

Bucer's conception of *disciplina* united the ethics of holiness drawn from the Ten Commandments and the headmasterly approach to the Christian community derived from the humanists. It entailed a restoration of Christian life and mores by an exterior system of penance and excommunication; the proper sanctification of churches and the Lord's Day; and the suppression of individual begging and almsgiving in favour of collective provision for those unable to work. He suggested the civil polity of the Spartans as the model for Christians to imitate: if one can use the word without offence, he represented in a strong form the tendency in all reformers to envisage the structure of the Church in a totalitarian spirit.

It was rather late in the day to be constructing a system of collective sanctification, and Bucer would have been surprised to discover that, ten years after his death, 'that word discipline' was in every mouth, *Books of Discipline* appearing from the presses north and south, and bodies of ministers and elders settling to their task. He would probably have smelled a rat, and with reason, since the moral universe of consistories, except perhaps in Calvin's Geneva, differed a good deal from his own. They were often in competition with civil jurisdictions which had taken advantage of the collapse of the canon law to annex the entire field of crime, dispute and personal violence to themselves. The Calvinist Electors of the Rhine Palatinate subsumed all these under the heading of offences which required reconciliation to the prince, leaving to their consistories only those requiring reconciliation to God. In Knox's Scottish *Book of Discipline* the actual definition of the term excluded matters already taken care of by the civil sword, and in Scotland, as to a lesser extent in England, a string of statutes reversed the policy of Pope Innocent III by making civil offences out of what had hitherto been sins. The implications of this became clear where, as in France, the civil power remained in more or less alien hands. The consistories of the Huguenot Cévennes, up in the mountains of Languedoc, were preoccupied with the entirely traditional concern of dispute and violence among the faithful, and seem to have been remarkably successful in establishing their communion as a quarterly love-day, or time of reconciliation. The ministers of Essex and Suffolk who formed the Dedham *classis* spent more of their meetings discussing the sacramental scheme of baptism, marriage and social communion than anything characteristically reformed. Their 'puritan' amendments to Cranmer's original design, as in baptism, look fairly marginal, and they failed to agree about two of the more striking symbols of reformed holiness, the strict sabbath and the conception of witchcraft as idolatry. The repression of blasphemy seems to have been low on everybody's agenda.

Still, it would be wrong to give the impression that discipline was nothing to get excited about. Like other inquisitorial systems, it caused a lot of trouble, put people off, and probably, as its opponents alleged, did more to divide parishes than to unite them. Its typically Calvinist effect of distinguishing the sheep from the goats was certainly welcome to many of the godly, who thought it unreasonable to bring together fire and water and then jib at the ensuing 'rumble'. Two positive general effects have been claimed for it, in both cases very plausibly; they sound contradictory. The first was the systematic working-out of the Ten Commandments as a code of actual behaviour, which gave Christian ethics a coherence it had lacked since the fourteenth century. The second, which may seem to hark back to aspects of medieval ethics, was a strong practical tendency to identify sin with fornication. This seems to have been especially true in Scotland, where sexual misdemeanour was the main issue in at least two-thirds of the cases dealt with by kirk sessions in the first half-century of discipline, and a long-term effect on the Scottish character, encouraging furtiveness and *tartufferie*, would be hard to dispute. As elsewhere, this was partly a consequence of the pre-emption of other moral territory by competing jurisdictions, but there must also have been a positive drift in this direction, since it seems in some degree a universal feature of the consistory regime: its stiffest penalties, which included a public confession of guilt, were always reserved for sexual offences. By way of reconciling these two effects, one might offer the thought that the conveyance to reformed populations of the ethics of holiness derived from the Ten Commandments was unlikely to be achieved except by reactivating the traditional instinct that holiness meant chastity. One might also observe that both of them were generally true of early modern Christianity. Tartuffe was not a Scottish Presbyterian.

In the end the need to provide Calvinist communities with a specific mark of visible holiness was appropriately met by the reinvention of the sabbath. Christian Sabbatarianism entailed the conviction that the commandment to keep the sabbath holy applied to the behaviour of Christians on the Lord's Day, and required total abstinence not only from work but from all profane recreations and pastimes, including those held lawful by other

Christians. Despised by Luther and Lutherans like Tyndale as a Jewish encumbrance and a violation of gospel freedom, gingerly treated by Calvin himself, and probably not much forwarded by Bucer's advocacy, it did not take hold of the imagination of Calvinists until after Calvin's death. It had some support from the ministry in France, but was chiefly propagated in the Rhineland Palatinate and among the Swiss. It reached Scotland during the 1570s, but had not fully taken hold of English Calvinists by the late 1580s, when it was the object of an unresolved dispute in the Dedham *classis*; they had adopted it by about 1600, and thereafter it became a universal mark of the Calvinist tradition.

The most influential account of Sabbatarianism has been that of Christopher Hill in *Society and Puritanism in Pre-Revolutionary England*. It has the peculiarity of arguing that the attractions of the Sabbatarian movement lay not in what it was saying about the sabbath, but in its implications for the rest of the week. But labouring on six days, though certainly part of the scriptural commandment, was surely not the main point. The sabbath was not viewed by its apostles as a method of work-discipline, and I doubt if it has ever been so viewed by those who have practised it. Its practical utility, for the dons of Heidelberg and Cambridge who advocated it, was mainly as an aid to catechism, since it had the effect of banning competitive activities on Sunday afternoons. There was also a theoretical connection, in that it was an example of the ten-commandment morality which catechisms were busy propagating. But the real force behind it came from elsewhere, and to see what it was we should think less about the six-day week and more about the situation of the Palatinate whence it came. In the later sixteenth century the Palatinate was a new and insecure Calvinist polity striving to get its head above the waters of Lutheranism and Catholicism which washed around it, in an environment where intelligible structures of popular Christian behaviour had often disintegrated. Holiness means separation; the sabbath, which was a ritual not a moral obligation, was a rite of separation. Calvinists, being called to holiness, needed such a rite even more than they needed rites of incorporation like the Eucharist; but the fathers of the Reformation, with their background of anti-ritual humanism, had left them with few resources in the area. They had abolished the separative aspects of baptism, and could not revive them, as the sects were to do, without raising the spectre of Anabaptism out of the grave. The rituals of iconoclasm, which had served in their time, were a wasting asset: after the orgy of the 1560s in the Netherlands there were not many vulnerable images left to be demolished. Fastings and exorcisms could be revived, but regular fasting (though enacted by a godly Parliament during the English Civil War) always smacked of popery. Meanwhile the sabbath could serve, week by week, to distinguish the sheep from the goats in the sort of establishment sectarianism which in England collapsed shortly after the ritual demolition of Cheapside Cross in 1642, precipitating English Calvinists into sectarianism proper.

I suppose it will seem paradoxical to have suggested that the history of Reformation ritual is an important subject; no more perhaps than to have offered the contrasting images of a Catholic discipline of the individual and his interior, and a reformed disicpline of the external and collective. They are not caricatures, but there is certainly more to be said. Counter-Reformation systems of private conversion were something of a monopoly of religious orders, and notably of the Jesuits; they accordingly inspired from the Catholic episcopate the competitive proposal of a reconstituted exterior discipline. Outlined in the 1530s by archaeologically minded bishops like Giberti of Verona, and not very successfully promoted at the Council of Trent, it came off the drawing-board in the episcopate of Carlo Borromeo in Milan, and passed thence to a string of bishops in northern Italy and, from 1600 onwards, in France. It probably also had some influence on the high profile of episcopacy cultivated by the Church of England during the reign of Charles I. As models of Christian discipline, Milan and Geneva had a great deal in common, and Borromeo was consciously competing for the palm of visible holiness with a city, after all, no great distance away. He seems to have thought the whole trend of the penitential system since 1215 a mistake. His ideal would have been to revive Lent as a season for the exercise of public penitential disciplines to be imposed in the sacrament: confession of sins would precede, and the reconciliation of the sinner follow, the penitential season, and the whole population would be purified in preparation for its Easter communion. The programme was not designed for popularity, and it is not altogether surprising that solid citizens of Milan tried to assassinate him. It could never be put into practice, but remained a gleam in the eye of the clergy, who could brandish it as a nightmare which might persuade the Catholic laity to submit to less rigorous control. This was the strategy of the French Jansenist clergy, who may have taken their doctrine from Jansen in Louvain but certainly got their discipline from Borromeo and Milan. Convinced as they were that the Jesuit recipe of devout self-awareness concealed a conspiracy with the laity to trivialise the sacrament, their version of the Borromean programme required an experimental period of practical conversion to supervene between the confession of sin and its absolution. Although it contradicted the general Counter-Reformation tendency towards more frequent confession and communion, it was widely influential among the secular clergy during the seventeenth and eighteenth centuries.

Jansenist confessional practice was the rather modest residuum of a vision of exterior discipline which never had a chance of finding a Catholic government willing to enforce it. For their part, and in not dissimilar circumstances, intending reformers of the English Church had already before 1600 begun to feel that the obsession with exterior discipline had been unfruitful, or at least, since it did not seem to be coming to pass in England, that they had better set about erecting a discipline within themselves. In this endeavour they had at the start to rely a good deal on Catholic spiritual writers, and the science of practical divinity, developed by William Perkins in Elizabethan Cambridge and perfected, as we shall see, by Richard Baxter after 1650, was a vernacular version of Catholic casuistry. They managed to give the tradition of the examination of conscience a new lease of life by infusing it with predestinarian theology, or at least with that version of it which dwelt upon the assurance which the godly man might feel of his election. Hence the multiplication during the seventeenth century of spiritual autobiographies which recounted the chain of experiences by which grace had come to convert and sanctify the soul. The puritan autobiographers had a model in St Augustine's *Confessions*, which had been kept in circulation mainly by Catholics; but their exploration of the interior life was characteristically of the Reformation in its sense of drama and dialectic, of the amazing interventions of grace. It is true that the genre declined into conventionality in the narratives of conversion required of aspirants to the congregational way of holiness, but in the mean time it had enabled John Bunyan to write at least one masterpiece, and according to some had given birth to the English novel. Unless we are to take as a late example of it the *Confessions* of Jean-Jacques Rousseau, it was not practised outside England. Like the Jansenists at the convent of Port-Royal, it was a symptom of *disciplina* in the desert.

On this reading, the confessional autobiography was indeed, as has often been said, an alternative to the sacramental confession of Catholics. But it may be a mistake to assume that it took the place of something which had been abolished at the Reformation: 'confession', too, was an early modern invention. Jesuits and Jansenists, rigorists and laxists, were in the end arguing about relatively minor practical consequences of a major event to which they were both (the latter, it is true, with some reluctance) committed: the transition in the sacrament from penance to *disciplina*, performed in the conviction that discipline was an interior process. If the conviction, among Catholics, seems to have had more force in seventeenth-century France than, say, in Spain, one reason was that public penitential performances had been much in evidence in the Catholicism of the League, which everybody now wished to forget. The visible symbol of this transition, or at least of its conveyance to the average Catholic, was the confessional-box, invented by Borromeo in 1565: this was another sleep-walking innovation, and a foundation-stone of modern Catholicism. No general law imposed it. It was adopted very gradually, and in many rural parishes unknown by 1650 or even 1700. Peasants, like the immortal Kate in Frank O'Connor's *First Confession*, found it hard to tell one end of it from the other.[15] It may seem perverse to connect the introduction of the confessional with the decay of penance, and this was certainly not Borromeo's intention, but two features of it ought to be make the connection clear. It more or less abolished the sacrament as a social ritual. By placing a barrier between the priest and the sinner, penetrable only by their disembodied murmurs, it made the *impositio manus*, or laying of the priest's hand upon the head of the penitent as a token of his reconciliation to God and his neighbour, impossible to perform. The effect was rather like leaving the water out of baptism. Some attempts were made, particularly it seems in southern Italy and Sicily, to devise a form of confessional which would not have this consequence, but the solutions sound rather absurd. For the most part the clergy either did not notice, or did not think it mattered. The installation of these solid and often impressive pieces of furniture against the pillars of old churches, their incorporation into the design of new ones, conveyed the positive message that repentance was a continuous business. Catholics might have been called to penance once a year, but were now to be called to confession all the year round.

New disciplinary systems, as the experience of the Huguenots of the Cévennes seems to show, were compatible with traditional conceptions of sin. But it would be implausible to suppose that so much radical upheaval of the machinery for dealing with guilt and forgiveness could occur without making a difference to what people were invited and likely to feel guilty about. It was bound, I think, in spite of the intentions of its authors, somewhat to diminish the consciousness that sin was principally embodied in defective human relations and sympathies. Of two possible alternatives we have caught sight of, one is obviously correct: almost everything, from the revival of the Ten Commandments downwards, conspired to enforce the conception that the proper description of sin was disobedience—disobedience to God, Church, king, to parents, teachers and authorities in general. During the sixteenth century, a moralised conception of obedience transformed the ethics of the English aristocracy, who had not had much time for it in the fifteenth; their history may serve as a model of something impinging, not always so successfully as in this case, on all sorts of people in all departments of the moral life. The humanists, who wanted all Christians to be 'religious', had certainly achieved something here.

The other possibility, an identification of sin with sexuality as such, is more questionable, though distinguished observers have argued for it. I have suggested that the moral statistics of some reformed Churches, which might be cited in favour of the idea, may actually prove something different; and that attitudes to conjugal sexuality became, if anything, somewhat more liberal. It was clearly true that the advent of *disciplina* throughout Christendom tended to mean a more continuous restraint upon the sexuality of the unmarried. One cannot see municipal authorities in the seventeenth century taking the view which many had held in the fifteenth, that the brothel was a Christian institution dedicated to the maintenance of social peace; the papacy, which against Protestant controversialists felt constrained to offer something like this defence for the existence of the stews of Rome, had rather covered itself with confusion. Since the seventeenth century seems to have been a period of declining premarital intercourse and a rising age of marriage, the restraint must have been considerable, and it seems academic to argue whether it entailed for the young more chastity or more masturbation. Either way a drift towards sexual obsession among the young seems plausible, though hardly proved. Catholic writers about confession were less obsessed than Protestants and liberals have tended to suppose, even if there may be something in Foucault's speculation that their heroic attention to the subject prepared the European mind to receive, in the end, a pan-sexual interpretation of human behaviour. Altogether the signs of disturbance on the sexual front do not seem to amount to a case that by 1700 Christians of any denomination were generally being taught or believed that sexual gratification occupied the centre of the universe of sin. They may have come nearer to this in the eighteenth century when, in Catholicism at least, a revival of naturalistic ethics began to make mountains of things like masturbation and contraception.

In *Paradise Lost,* the consummation of a whole European genre of epic representations of the drama of sin and salvation, Sin was a sorceress, head-sprung daughter and lover of the rebellious Satan, mother of Death. Milton's invention will surely carry authority as an image of sin in the age of the Commandments. It also tells us much of what we need to know about the history of the witch since she had emerged in the fifteenth century as an enemy of the human race, and about why the innovation had proved so persuasive in the century before Milton wrote. It had certainly bred death on a large scale; not quite so large as has usually been supposed, but larger than confessional persecution as such. The facts about the witch-panic are roughly as follows. Still a comparatively insecure novelty during the decades between the publication of the *Malleus maleficarum* and the Reformation, the new model of witchcraft took another lease of life around 1560, and inspired widespread, continuous and obsessive concern for some three-quarters of a century. After about 1630, panics and waves of repression became more occasional, though not less severe when they occurred, until the end of the century. There were none after 1700 except in parts of eastern Europe. We do not need to be surprised that the firmest affirmation of the real existence of the syndrome was made by one of the greatest of sixteenth-century intellects, Jean Bodin (*Démono-manie des sorciers*, 1580), for Bodin believed in the Ten Commandments with a passion which seems to have converted him from Christianity to Judaism. In so far as everybody now took the Commandments to be the fundamental statement of Christian ethics, everybody believed in the new-model witch. If she had not already existed they would have had to invent her.

To know how the Devil was worshipped, one needed only to know what true religion was, and turn it inside out. Early Protestants had little difficulty in envisaging the details of the cult, since the mass provided so obvious a model. Catholics took this as a compliment, and their confidence that they knew what went on at the witches' 'sabbaths' increased as predictions about the travesty of their own liturgy seemed to be confirmed by the confessions of culprits. Through the looking-glass one passed, to quote a Spanish friar, from sacraments to excrements; instead of kissing the pax at mass, one kissed the Devil's arse, and things like that. Possibly sensitive to the force of the argument, later Protestants tended to the older view that the main item in the cult was the anti-baptism or diabolic pact which would be revealed by marks on the person who had gone through it; but evidence on both points was readily accepted by either party. The model diffused itself mainly in a northern direction, from the western parts of the Empire and the eastern parts of France, to the Netherlands, the English-speaking world, and Scandinavia; it maintained its influence in the alpine and Pyrenean regions, without apparently much increasing it; it caught on to some extent in northern Italy, and not at all in Spain. The later alarms occurred in notably marginal places: England (1640s), Scotland (1640s, 1690s), Sweden (1660s), Massachusetts (1690s), Poland (eighteenth century); none occurred on the Celtic fringe. Until a late date the English continued to maintain the traditional view that witchcraft meant only maleficence. The main body of writing on the subject was composed in Germany, France and England between 1570 and 1630.

In accounting for the phenomenon, which historians have made more of a meal of than they need have done, the chief question is why a conception invented in the religious and intellectual climate of the fifteenth century should have been found convincing in the radically altered climate of the sixteenth and seventeenth. Its fabulous character, so distinctive to late medieval thinking about

Christianity, would not, one might have thought, have recommended it to reformers; and there were indeed some, like the Englishman Reginald Scot (*The Discoverie of Witchcraft*, 1584), for whom the exploits of witches belonged in the same category of mental rubbish as the wonders alleged of the saints. His Catholic contemporary Montaigne felt much the same. But they were evidently exceptional. Most of their contemporaries accepted that the collective fable represented an undeniable truth, somewhat as Lutherans and others accepted the fifteenth-century version of the Holy Family, without necessarily believing the story of the Holy House at Loreto. As Carnival was the inverted image of the traditional machinery of penance, the behaviour of the new-model witch was the inverted image of a moral system founded on the Ten Commandments, and particularly of the first table. The Devil, who had been the mirror-image of Christ, the personified principle of the hatred of one's neighbour, became a mirror-image of the Father, the focus of idolatry, and hence of uncleanness and rebellion. His status had been much enhanced by the translation, which left a sizeable space in the moral universe for Antichrist to fill. The witch was one who worshipped the Devil, blasphemed the Lord and inverted the sabbath before inverting all the other commandments. If she was usually a woman, it was partly because the traditional witch was usually a woman, and partly because Christian worship was conducted by males.

In presenting this conception of witchcraft to sixteenth-century Christendom, the voice of authority was more or less united, just as it was about catechism: indeed the witch-syndrome was something like a strip-cartoon version of catechism. Hence I think it gets the matter a little off-centre to see the repression of witchcraft, as Trevor-Roper has done, as principally a function of the conflict of confessional establishments; it was certainly stimulated by their competitive anxiety to prove holiness, but that seems rather different. In contrast to this unanimity of the learned, the unlearned seem extremely confused. On the whole their assumption was that witches performed malefice, and that malefice was something to be afraid of. Now they were being told, by and large, that witches were a very serious matter, but malefice was not; that it was either a contingent offshoot of graver matters, or actually impossible. In Württemberg and elsewhere in Lutheran Germany, theologians were advising them that witches could not actually do them harm (if they suffered harm it was the fault of their own sins), though for his own purposes the Devil might have persuaded the malicious that they could. This was not much consolation to people who had been warned off a variety of useful aids like holy water and were probably on that account feeling particularly sensitive to malice in their neighbours. One must suppose that, in all denominations, continuous preaching and catechising genuinely convinced a fair number of pious people of the modern view, persuading them not to take thought for themselves but to search out furiously the enemies of God. It certainly persuaded quite a lot of children, who provided much of the evidence in the seventeenth century. Perhaps they did not need to be so pious: the new idea of the Devil obviously caught on more readily than the new idea of God. On the other hand many people were simply working off traditional feelings by bringing against suspected enemies such charges as they thought would go down best with the jurisdiction to which they were offered. Under the statute law of Henry VIII and Charles V, so far as that obtained in the Empire, simple malefice would do; most judges were looking for something racier. One's judgement on the place of the new witchcraft in the popular history of Christian morals will depend on which of these responses one thinks the stronger. My own impression is that the invention did not do much to resolve the confusion it had created, or have much effect either in superseding the ethics of charity, or in establishing those of holiness. Catechism, though duller, made more difference in the long run.

While not a decisive episode in the history of sin, the witch-craze has a good deal to say about the death of penance. The passage from 'restitutive' to 'abstract' justice has rightly been described as the legal issue in the passage from one conception of witchcraft to another, and it accounts for much of the divergence on the subject between the learned and the population. In Christianity, the name for restitutive justice is penance. Applied to traditional penitential matter, the ideas of the victimless crime, sin in the mind and truth by self-accusation could pave the way to *metanoia* or to extermination, but not to penance. This seems to be why the witch-craze made so little headway in Spain, or in Mediterranean Europe as a whole. The Spaniards are supposed to have been preserved by the scepticism of their inquisitors, as indeed they were in a fairly crucial case in 1614. But what the Inquisition meant in this instance, as the witch-hunter Pierre de Lancre observed crossly from over the border, was a traditional practice of penance, a traditional notion of sin, and innocence of *disciplina*. It would be worth enquiring whether, by courtesy of the Church courts, something of the same sort did not occur in England.

(iii) Charity

On all sides, during the first decades of the Reformation, dedicated people sought to establish the Eucharist as the centre of the consciousness of Christians and of social unity. Luther offered a version of the mass which represented the unifying sacrament without the divisive sacrifice; Zwingli designed a social community of remembrance, invited to take Christ into its heart by assembling around a table in imitation of the Last Supper. Calvin expounded with great eloquence the bond of brotherhood in the body of Christ, and some of his successors proved better than he did at getting a sense of this into their liturgy. Cranmer tried the German way and then the Swiss, in search of a ritual which would bring unity to the commonwealth. All reformers looked for an intenser communion through mutual participation in the cup. For their part Catholics and Anabaptists revived, in different forms, the kiss of peace.

Considering that they were building on a solid layer of familiar quasi-eucharistic institutions of eating and drinking, in church and out of it, their efforts ought to have been rewarded. It is fairly obvious that they were not; by, say, 1650 few reformed communities had managed to create a symbol of social unity as powerful as the Host, or a celebration of togetherness as popular as the feast of Corpus Christi. Why was this? A multitude of good reasons spring to mind, so many that one is driven to wonder whether the passionate intensity with which a higher eucharistic unity was canvassed in the years from 1520 to 1560 did not indicate, rather than a new beginning, some final spasm of the pre-Reformation theme of sacred society. The primacy of the perspicuous word over the mysteriously integrative rite, of faith over charity, were in themselves the fissiparous forces which nervous conservatives diagnosed. I do not know that they are sufficient to account for the instant inability of the first reformers to agree on a theology and practice of the Eucharist, so that, to quote Bucer's colleague in

Strassburg, Wolfgang Capito, they became hopelessly divided by the one symbol which should have united them. Given more flexibility, particularly on Luther's part, agreement might possibly have been reached at Marburg in 1529. But even if it had been, it is hard to see it achieving the effect desired. There seems something inherently unreasonable about raising the standard of community as high as the reformers were doing, and expecting entire populations to live up to it for more than a couple of days in the year, and without the assistance of alcohol. Luther seems to have been aware of this from the start, seeing communion fulfilled in a voluntary domestic eucharist and in nothing much larger, Christians being as few as they were. The higher ambitions of Bucer and Calvin succumbed—in Calvin's case it would almost seem on purpose—to the seeming fatality whereby reformed rituals of society transformed themselves into rituals of exclusion.

The history of the Eucharist after the Reformation is more than a history of the misfortunes of reformers. More or less everybody was affected by the heresy which loomed at the further end of the Christianity of the spirit: that the union to be sought was with that other spirit, God, not with that tiresome incarnation your neighbour. This was certainly not what Zwingli meant when he chose for his eucharistic message the text that the flesh profited nothing, but his Christ in the mind was rather easily separable from Christ the social body; as easily perhaps as the Christ in the heart of Thomas à Kempis's interior dialogue. It was almost certainly the latter which had the larger influence, by encouraging the private eucharist of asocial mysticism which was eventually to become the Holy Communion of modern and subcontemporary Catholicism. It also probably lay behind Luther's conception of the Eucharist as a pledge of peace and forgiveness to the individual soul which, with his doctrine of the real presence, inspired a devotional tradition not very different from that of the Counter-Reformation. It may well have given strength to the second person singular in which, to the irritation of many, communion in the new English rite continued to be administered. The assumption by seventeenth-century French devotional writers that the customary *Pax* was better represented by the cultivation of private sentiments than by an exterior ritual act testifies to their desire to promote interior feelings which might be jeopardised by actual contact with one's neighbour. Their idea of a spiritual communion was not the same as Zwingli's, nor was their idea of the Sacred Heart what Cranmer meant by 'feed on him in thine heart by faith', but all of them were one way and another expressing a eucharistic feeling in which the emotional prevailed over the social.

One consequence of devotional privacy, seemingly local to England, had been the invention of the pew, 'a certain place in church incompassed with wainscot or some other thing' where the gentry could get a bit of peace to pursue their devotions during mass. Richard Gough, who composed his social history of Myddle in Shropshire as a commentary on the ownership and distribution of the pews in its church, recorded about 1700 that the tradition there was that pews had come in with the Reformation, since people needed somewhere to sit while lessons were being read and sermons preached. But pews were for kneeling as well as for sitting, and Gough knew that the chief inhabitants of Myddle had had them since before the Reformation. The effect of the change of religion in most of the churches he knew had been to generalise the invention, leaving the entire floor-space, a century and a half later, covered with rows of pews or benches, with aisles or alleys for access. In England the pew prevailed over the bench or form; it represented, more or less, the distribution of households or 'families' in the parish and erected appropriate barriers between them. It was an invention as momentous as the division of the churchyard into family plots, with which it was roughly contemporary. Had there been no Reformation, it would have put an end to church-feasting, to the *Pax*, and to most of the traditional rites of Christian integration. It did not of course put an end to communion, but it certainly scuppered attempts to domesticate a Zwinglian eucharist in England by placing a communion table in the centre of churches. In short, the English parish church of the late seventeenth century embodied the conception of public worship as an assembly of segregated households portrayed, perhaps ironically, by Thomas More in *Utopia*. No other reformed Church seems to have gone quite so far as this, but all required seats for hearing the Word (or commonly, in the first century or so, for going to sleep), and few found a convincing place for a communion table.

The history of the furnishing of Catholic churches is more obscure: supposing the tendency towards pewing had started outside England, it must have been stopped by the Counter-

Reformation. Benches, however, spread across church floors during the seventeenth century. They were required at the front by the gentry, who had been driven by the clergy out of the choir, though they were often still entrenched in their chapels; by catechists, by preachers, and possibly by those who advocated the segregation of men and women on different sides of the church. Borromeo's device of a wooden barrier for this purpose down the middle of churches does not seem to have caught on, but by the eighteenth century Catholic churches were probably almost as covered with seating as Protestant ones, their mass-attenders separated almost as firmly from one another as the priest from the penitent by the confessional-box. Dominated by pulpit and altar, encumbered by more or less permanent erections of timber, churches of all denominations could now scarcely be anything else but places of spiritual communion.

It has been said of Zwingli's eucharist that it was a testimony to pre-existing unity rather than a means of creating it. Though the testimony is less evident in Catholic and Lutheran practice, the assumption was rather the same, that social unity could be left to look after itself, or was safe in the hands of civility or the State. That growing conviction, which had surely become established among the educated by 1700, consigned the Eucharist of tradition to obsolescence. It was confirmed by the effects of confessional plurality where that existed, and by the consequent emergence after 1650 of the idea of civil society. It entailed a displacement of the theory and practice of charity.

The place of charity in the scheme of salvation had been a contentious issue in Reformation and anti-Reformation theology. But since both parties, in the end, came round to much the same view of the subject we may treat the controversy about faith and works as, in this respect, tangential to a shift already well under way by 1520. Through the diffusion both of Renaissance civility and of Renaissance activism, the state of enlarged sociability, which was what Augustine and the medieval Church had principally meant by charity, lost persuasiveness as a high object of Christian aspiration and a condition of the salvation of those who participated in it.

It would be idyllic to suppose that medieval charity was a relationship into which money did not much enter. But it was not relevant to the majority of situations where charity was in question, and all the 'corporal works of mercy' (feeding, clothing, hospitality, visiting the sick and imprisoned, burying the dead) could perfectly well be carried on without any money changing hands. This was in keeping with the sensible if unheroic view expressed in the canon law that charity was better directed to those with whom one was in some actual relation (that is, to one's kin or neighbours) than to perfect strangers. By 1400, it is true, the most recorded form of charity to one's relations did involve money, since it was mainly through payment for masses or indulgences that the dead could be benefited. It was held at the Reformation, and has since been agreed by nervous Catholic historians, that the sense of charitable obligation to one's kin in purgatory took money which would otherwise have gone to relieve the corporal wants of one's common Christian neighbour. The rise of purgatory probably had a depressing effect on the endowment of hospitals, although these were until the fifteenth century intended more for the pious traveller than for the sick. But calculations of public utility seem foreign to the ethos of medieval charity. Family obligations fulfilled, those who had money preferred to spent it in benefactions by which a more personal connection with the meritorious poor, suffering or otherwise Christ-like, could be created. It went to the beggar in the street, the poor at the kitchen door, the recipient of the funeral dole. Large or impersonal benefactions were more usually the product of penance or panic than acts of charity as such, since almsdeeds formed one of the authorised ways whereby satisfaction could be made for sin. They were likely to be prescribed in cases of avarice or usury. Yet here too the authoritative opinion, represented by John Geiler in the early sixteenth century, was that if a known individual had been damaged restitution must be made to him personally. Abstract benefaction to the poor in general might meet the obligation of penance, but not the obligation of charity, which was to actual persons. It seems from the contents of wills that the doctrine was in fact put into practice, if only by people on their death-beds.

It was by the 1520s a distinctly old-fashioned view, having been superseded among the more up-to-date by a concept of charity which discountenanced any actual connection between the benefactor and the receiver. 'The idea of *caritas*', it has been said of Florence around 1400, 'was transvalued into a generalised concept of philanthropy.'[16] Though the word is anachronistic, the concept seems to have become established in the writings of Florentine humanists of the fifteenth century. It implied a feeling for active but abstract benevolence or *humanitas* as a duty of the citizen, a civilised disgust for beggars, a hostility to many of the relationships which had hitherto been supposed especially to entail mutual charity, and a particular contempt for friars. The new philanthropy did not have things all its own way during the fifteenth century, even in Italy. Against the new wave of more systematic or more ambitious hospital foundations following Brunelleschi's Florentine *Ospedale degli Innocenti* of the 1420s ought to be set the *monti di pietà*, an important development of the traditional view of charity sustained by the friars and their anti-Semitic hearers.

By 1500 or so the abstract view of charity had passed from civic humanists to civic patriciates and was spreading from Italy to the north. One of its symptoms was the reconstruction of the smarter fraternities in such a way that their charity came to consist less in how their members behaved to each other, and more in what they or their officers did on behalf of defined categories of needy outsiders. In Genoa, home of that early model of the saint in hospital administration, Caterina Fieschi (1447–1510), the Oratory of Divine Love was a conscious embodiment of the new philanthropy. In Venice it mostly slipped in unnoticed while endowments for purposes of public benevolence accumulated in trust funds deposited with the long-established penitential fraternities, the *Scuole Grandi*. In the cause of administering these funds efficaciously the *Scuole* developed an oligarchical character resented by many of their members; they also felt the need to erect such unascetic premises as those built for the *Scuola* of San Rocco during the 1580s and decorated, impressively but somehow unfraternally, by Tintoretto. Another sign of the times was the passage of hostility to begging into an aggressive phase. This can be traced in the expansion of one category of idealised poor, the *poveri vergognosi* who were ashamed to beg, as well as in the drift of city administrators towards the banning of begging, and of individual almsgiving to beggars, altogether. This radical breach with Catholic tradition was nevertheless the point of departure for the model system of collective municipal philanthropy designed for the city of Ypres by the humanist Juan Luis Vives in 1527 and taken up more or less complete by a string of Catholic cities during the 1530s. By then it had been fallen upon with a good deal of glee by the reformers, and perhaps particularly by those among them who were refugees from the mendicant orders. Bucer held that both begging and individual almsgiving contaminated the holiness of the godly community; his vesting of public welfare in a congregational diaconate was imitated by Calvin, with the unintended result that in post-Reformation Holland only the minority of the population which belonged to the Reformed Church was entitled to it. Normally, however, in both Catholic and Protestant territories, the function was taken over or strictly supervised by the civil power. The upshot of the civic philanthropy of the early fifteenth-century Florentine humanists was the rigorously bureaucratic, all-inclusive, tax-supported Welfare State erected by the Medici as Grand Dukes of Tuscany a century or so later.

This was not a necessary outcome. It has been argued that in England the public welfare machinery erected by statute in the Poor Laws of 1530 and after made a modest contribution to the relief of the poor and disabled, compared with institutions erected by the spontaneous benevolence of Protestant Englishmen. The danger here would be to create a dichotomy between public and private which would not have occurred to anybody at the time, and to damage the substantial unity of the conception of charity which came to dominate early modern Europe. The prohibition of begging, and discouragement of giving to beggars, signified its arrival because it symbolised the decay of the notion that reciprocity and some kind of personal relation (on the beggar's part, praying for the soul of his benefactor) were necessary characteristics of an act of charity. It intimated that there was such a thing as an act of charity which did not need a state of charity to take place in.

The conception of charity as activity had by the middle of the sixteenth century received two distinct embodiments. Its Catholic form was a fairly direct product of Renaissance activism, and chiefly represented by the Society of Jesus (1540), though the Society's founder, Ignatius Loyola, had probably intended something rather different. It looked for the highest expression of charity to large, efficiently managed and heroically executed works directed to saving the soul, improving the mind, and relieving the corporal needs of a rather abstract and rather passive neighbour. In its Protestant form, it emerged from the doctrine of charity resorted to by the early reformers when defending themselves against the charge that they were drying up the springs of Christian charity altogether. Their claim was that true faith would be known by its fruits, one of which would be the production of 'works of charity'. Since giving to the individual living or praying for the individual dead were no longer respectable, these were practically bound to be impersonal or 'durable' works like schools and almshouses. They also claimed that the charitable Christian, being no longer required to support such futile or vicious causes as the souls in purgatory or the mendicant orders, would be in a position to give a great deal more to such genuine works in future. Their predictions seem to have been borne out by the contents of English wills in the century after the Reformation.

These two traditions invoked contrasting theologies of salvation, and had some fairly important incidental differences. To judge by statistics of literacy, the second of the traditional 'spiritual works of mercy', the instruction of the ignorant, was better provided for by Protestants. On the benefactors' side, the attention of Catholics seems to have been almost wholly directed to the executant, that of Protestants to the donor. The survival in Catholicism of the extremely adaptable model of the religious order or congregation made for a different sociology of charitable activity. Where this encouraged specialisation, as with the Brothers of St John of God who after 1600 took as their vocation the care of the insane, it may have produced a higher standard of professional skill. But in substance, and by comparison with the conception of charity they superseded, the two varieties of activism seem effectively the same. Both were products of a century disposed to risk, like Calvin in his revaluation of the usury taboo, dismantling the actual relations of Christians in the hope of procuring some more general benefit for the Christian community as a whole.

One of its most learned historians, Eduardo Grendi, has described the new philanthropy as a 'useful myth', but this is surely too dismissive. Of the good it did, it seems enough to say that by accident or design it helped to pull the West through its first period of exceptional human distress since the fourteenth century, and that in its durable provision of schools, hospitals and systematic poor relief it erected something more than the foundations of the modern Welfare State. Its untoward consequences were equally extensive. The moral confusion caused as its principles filtered down to the average housewife has been held to have exacerbated the phobia about witches; and certainly the inability of poor old women to respond to material generosity with privileged prayers for the soul of the giver left them without much to contribute to Christian society except malefice. Value for money, the decay of reciprocity, a sense that God had somehow transferred his favour from the poor to the rich, were dark shadows thrown by the erection of the edifice of professional charity. They led with apparent inevitability to the *Grand Renfermement* or Great Incarceration diagnosed by Michel Foucault in the later seventeenth century: the segregation in rigorously administered institutions of all those incarnations of the stranger to whom charity was now thought to be especially due.

Except perhaps in the final denouement, which was here postponed, English practice had fairly faithfully followed Continental: the enactment and provisions of Poor Law statutes from Thomas Cromwell onwards exemplified humanist anti-mendicant principles and the difficulties of enforcing them. The shift towards closed institutions was embodied in the beginnings of the English workhouse, whose native model, the London Bridewell, was the least sympathetic of the five London hospitals erected or refounded after the dissolution of the monasteries. It took them some time to discover their special vocations, and Continental inspiration or simple competition seems to be visible in an Act of 1624 encouraging the foundation of more 'hospitals, maisons de diew . . . or houses of correction'. Through the badging of the poor and similar marks of distinction, charity proceeded as elsewhere from a mode of relation to a mode of segregation. The relation between public provision and private benefaction, though certainly a contrast with the Welfare State in Tuscany, seems little different from that prevailing in Venice, apart from the presence there of the mediating *Scuole* whose English counterparts the Reformation had abolished.

Partly because begging refused to be suppressed, domestic relief, which at least for those considered meritorious characterised the humanist schemes of the 1530s, began to be overtaken by the closed institution. During the twenty years after 1600 a string of comprehensive constructions began to be erected in Amsterdam, Paris, Lyon, Florence and elsewhere. Thereafter the immense influence of Vincent de Paul (whose genial invention of the *Filles de la Charité* in 1633 recruited the poor in the service of the poor and had the exceptional effect of uniting more efficiency with more humanity) carried the Counter-Reformation tradition of institutional charity through to such massive establishments as the *Albergo dei Poveri* at Genoa, opened in 1664. This broad coincidence may seem a point in favour of historians, like Keith Wrightson, who have seen the motive for the transformations of charity as lying outside Christianity, in a context of demographic problems and nervous class relations; so might a chronology which seems to point to the years around 1620 as critical. The alternative view, which I share, would allege the substantial continuity, homogeneity and interior logic of a process extending over at least 150 years, for whose pulsations Continental historians have given up trying to find correlatives in the demographic conjuncture, the class struggle or the price of grain. It would also give a great deal of weight to questions of definition and classification, especially in the segregation of new categories of the afflicted, for whose needs only a lurid or insensitive imagination could make 'Society' responsible. One of these was the insane, the story of whose charitable incarceration has been written by Foucault. Whether or not poverty was creating piety in Protestant Essex, piety unquestionably, in the form of the Brothers of St John of God, created in 1645 the *Charité* or madhouse of Charenton, whose most famous inmate was to be the Marquis de Sade.

If we are looking for a brave attempt at a statement of what had happened to Western Christianity as a social regime, where anything had happened, in the preceding century or two, we can find it in a folio volume of more than 1,000 pages first published in 1673 by the Englishman Richard Baxter: *A Christian Directory; or a Summ of Practical Theologie and Cases of Conscience.* This may seem an Anglocentric view; but the international scrutiny to which Baxter's work has been submitted since the publication of Max Weber's *Protestant Ethic* in 1904 seems a just reflection of Baxter's ambition and achievement. He was of course an English Protestant writing in English for Englishmen, but he was also in his own context something like a universal man. He was dedicated, in an age when most people had given it up, to the unity of English Protestantism, to the reconciliation of episcopacy and presbytery, of liturgy and the word. In fundamental theology he began his career as a predestinarian and finished it an Arminian. His field was practical divinity or the theology of Christian behaviour, a region where confessional polemic was rarely appropriate; and he was perfectly aware that, behind the succession of English practical divines in which he had his place, there was a larger, Continental and principally Catholic tradition which any man with his ambitions must treat as an ally. His claim to stand in this larger tradition is evident from his title.

Baxter's sum of practical divinity amounted to a comprehensive restatement of the obligations of Christian behaviour. It was intended to supplant the traditional frame of mind, not exactly by dethroning charity from its seat of primacy, but by rewriting the obligation of charity—as it had in practice been rewritten during the past two centuries—as an obligation of activity on behalf of the neighbour in general. Christian behaviour was characterised as obedience to the Commandments, and among them to the first table before the second; the criterion of a moral action was whether the question of obedience was raised by it. But there was more to obedience than conformity to exact precepts, important as these were; the end of moral action was the glory of God and the diffusion of holiness. The classical statement of the duties of the true Christian was the parable of the talents, which required from him spontaneous and creative moral activity. Baxter's 'servant' was not so much God's employee as God's agent. Christianity, as one of Baxter's precursors, Richard Sibbes, had put it, was a busy trade. Charity in particular was work: it was 'doing all the good we can to others'. This was a charter for durable works to the benefit of Church and commonwealth, for social work rather than human relations.

True, Baxter made a distinction between charity and the works of charity, and one part of the book was a perfectly traditional exposition of the obligations of actual neighbourhood. But charity in this historic sense did not come under Christian ethics but Christian politics, nor does it seem to have had much to contribute to the glory of God. Baxter's strong feeling for the duty of peace and concord had been almost wholly absorbed in the task of reconciling the denominations and preaching against sectarianism. In ordinary relations the cultivation of friendship (which he enjoyed), and even of civility, worried him greatly as a hindrance to God's work. He had no place for kinship, real or artificial, beyond the edification of the domestic family, and even then he thought that pastors of the Church should not marry. With some exception for the godly, all his brothers were others.

In offering the *Christian Directory* as a summa of two centuries of revisionary but transconfessional thought and practice about charity, I am conscious that Baxter is commonly given a different role. As founder of a 'Protestant ethic' held to have shaped the modern world, he will no doubt continue to be blessed or cursed by generations of sociology students yet unborn. Neither a close reading of Baxter's text, nor a sense of its context, will inspire much confidence that the picture is a true likeness. Of the three elements of the Protestant ethic claimed to be present in his book, the obligation of diligence in a worldly calling is certainly there, though subordinate to the conventional obligations of religion: Baxter's activism did not, as it had sometimes done for Jesuits, dismantle the barrier between secular occupations and works of piety and charity. Again, his favourite moral concept, redeeming the time ('because the days are evil'), meant something more eschatological than not wasting time at the office, though it sometimes meant that too. As between diligent Martha and Christ-obsessed Mary, Mary was the one who was redeeming the time. Finally, the only justification for growing rich by 'worldly ascet-ism' was to be able to devote the product to durable works of piety and charity like maintaining the ministry, evangelising the heathen, or founding a university in Wales: in short to 'do good'.

About Baxter himself, that is probably all that needs to be said; about his posterity, and that of the Promethean view of charity which he represented, there seems something more to say. The suggestion has been offered by T. C. Smout that the remarkable achievements of eighteenth-century Scots might be regarded as a posthumous effect of the Christian activism preached by the Kirk after sanctification, its original purpose, had ceased to appeal. The idea, which is not so far from Weber's, seems worth a wider airing. My own guess would be that when Baxter died in 1691 the heroic theory of good works was getting mixed up in people's minds with mercantilist economics, creating an ethos of public benefaction in which, among others, the entrepreneur might feel more at home than hitherto. This mixture would not in itself constitute a *Protestant* ethic, since both its elements were at least as vigorous in Colbert's France, say, as in England. There would, however, be the difference that in Reformation Christianity the doctrine of social work had been preached while the provision for social workers, outside the ministry and the teaching profession, had been neglected. The religious orders of the Counter-Reformation, now at the height of their multiple activities, still kept the vocation to do good in well-established channels; Protestants may well have been driven to take their vocations elsewhere. In defence of such speculations, as indeed of Weber's, it can be held that they explore a region where speculation is hardly to be avoided. The region of the translations of Christianity is a region of historical darkness, and the translation which Weber tried to put his finger on is not the only one lurking there.

8 Migrations of the Holy

(i) The State

Some years before the Reformation Thomas More, having made his decision for the civil and against the religious life, had attempted a discussion of Christian politics in the guise of a life of King Richard III. His story would have made sense to Émile Durkheim. The community of Christian Englishmen, one could deduce, was kept in existence by a complex of holy things of which the most important were the sacraments and the most visible a certain number of places and objects. The duty of a Christian king was to offer to these things a due respect himself and to inculcate it in others. King Edward IV had performed these duties, in particular by expounding most eloquently on his death-bed the Christian character of matrimonial affinity. King Richard had not. The critical moments in More's story were not acts of usurpation, not even perhaps acts of murder, but acts in violation of the holy: of the sanctity of holy places in Richard's removal of his brother's son from sanctuary, and of the sanctity of his brother's marriage. The clergy, whose duty was to be a living embodiment of the sacred, had through worldliness connived at these violations. At the centre of community there had opened an abysmal void. More's history was left without a denouement, which Henry VIII was shortly to provide. Meanwhile Acts of Parliament against sanctuary and benefit of clergy abolished or restricted the immunity of holy places and 'spiritual' persons. They were modest enough in themselves but, like the agitation for the reform of marriage law in France and elsewhere, they showed that More's preoccupations were no longer widely shared among the educated and law-abiding laity. After 1530 public opinion accepted without much difficulty Henry's more systematic destruction of historic sanctities, and More was left to meditate in the Tower on the coming of the Turk.

Divorces between the sacred and the body social were to be everyday events in the sixteenth century. Luther gave them a constitutional warrant by his radical dismissal of incarnate holiness, and by his dictum that marriage was not a subject it was proper for the clergy to get mixed up in. His doctrine of the two kingdoms appeared to mean that the social world was in any case the province of the Devil, and if the Devil chose, as was more than likely, to be represented by such as Richard III and Henry VIII, Christians would have to grin and bear it. In this respect More and Luther had more in common than either would probably have conceded. Luther's doctrine of the providential role of the temporal kingdom, and of the divine ordinance of submission to it, was certainly an important reinforcement of the authority of rulers, as Henry himself remarked of the version of it presented to him by William Tyndale (*The Obedience of a Christian Man*, 1528). But that is not to say that Luther thought the State was holy, or encouraged others to think so. It seems a mistake to claim, as J. N. Figgis did, that he 'transferred to the temporal sovereign the halo of sanctity that had hitherto been mainly the preserve of the ecclesiastical', and to see in him a forerunner of Rousseau or Hitler. It is true that Luther had a knack of inspiring conclusions which he claimed not to have intended, and there may be something of this here. But neither he nor More can have predicted, and I cannot believe that Luther would have welcomed, the strength of the current of respectable Christian opinion which was to place kings and their office within the sacred circle erased from so many other points of the social landscape.

Had they been Frenchmen they might have seen this outcome as distinctly on the cards. The successful conclusion of the Hundred Years War had stimulated a political cult which, by borrowing a good deal of the ritual of the feast of Corpus Christi, annexed to the profit of monarchy the most powerful sacred symbol in Christianity. While Richard III was still reigning in England, King Charles VIII of France had been received by the citizens of Rouen with something like a secular mass. Taking advantage of the fact that the arms of their city displayed the *Agnus Dei*, they exploited the sources of relevant symbolism available in both the mass and the text of the Apocalypse. They described their young and otherwise unattractive king as Lamb of God, saviour, head of the mystical body of France, guardian of the book with seven seals, fountain of life-giving grace to a dry people, deified bringer of peace; one worthy to receive, without the formality of being slain, blessing and honour, glory and power.[17] This transposition of Van Eyck's celebrated altar-piece at Ghent, *The Adoration of the Lamb*, would probably have been found scandalous in England, though tendencies in the same direction may be detected around the Burgundian dukes and the imperial Habsburgs. In France, reinforced by the holy phial of coronation oil and the royal touch for scrofula, hallowed by a martyr in the still disputable person of Joan of Arc, it crowned a formidable edifice of sacred royalty. By the accession of Francis I in 1515 it had become comparatively banal to speak of the king of France as a corporeal god.

If one could go as far as this within the Gothic universe whose complications exercised the ingenuity of composers of public spectacle around 1500, one could go a good deal further after traditional pieties had been devastated by humanist classicism. Any student of the civil law knew that the majesty of emperors was sacred, and a lawyer who had read the master of French legal humanism, Guillaume Budé, could think of himself as a priest officiating at the rites of majesty. To anyone with a decent humanist education it was a fact of elementary vocabulary that civil peace fell into the category of sacred things. In this climate a perfectly secular sort of sacred was asking to be created; it was created by Jean Bodin during the 1570s, and its name was sovereignty.

Bodin, it has been held, was by conviction a Jew, and there may therefore be some question about presenting his *Six livres de la république* as evidence of a geological shift in Christian conceptions of the relation between the sacred and the body social or politic. But, if a Jew, he was undoubtedly what the music-hall Irishman would call a Catholic Jew. His origins, like Calvin's, lay in those parts of northern France which were deeply attached to conventional pieties, and refused to have any truck with the Reformation while preserving a marked indifference to initiatives of Catholic spirituality. How much of this got into his political activity is disputed; in the *Six livres* it came out in a chapter on corporate institutions, communes and gilds. These, he held, were embodiments of Christian association, expressions of friendship, alliance and mutual love. He recognised that they also entailed faction and sedition, but even in the trying circumstances of 1576, when

Catholic corporatism was becoming a political nightmare, he showed himself more sympathetic to it than to the organised forces of political Protestantism. He thought it possible for a fraternally constructed community to exist on a comparatively large scale, as it did among the Swiss. It would settle its disputes by arbitration, though lacking a sovereign it could not be called a commonwealth. (If he had lived to see the unfortunate Confederation erected by the Catholic Irish in 1641 he might have changed his mind, but then the Irish seem less well adapted to confederation than the Swiss.) Well-advised governments would not dismantle such institutions, but prudently encourage them so as to diffuse mutual amity among their citizens, and see to their representation in a parliament or body of Estates.

But institutions of fraternity were, to say the least, not the main preoccupation of the *Six livres*, and it is not obvious that he thought of them as connected with any religious impulse. Bodin's notion of religion was central to his thought, and exemplifies a phase in the history of that word of which something will be said later; it was nearer to Calvin's than to traditional usage. Religion for him was a 'contemplative' virtue amounting to reverence for what ought to be revered: it was both the formal object of social arrangements and an indispensable aid in the preservation of commonwealths, but it was not exactly a social virtue in itself. Its substantive obligations had been codified for all time in the Ten Commandments, whence Bodin, like most contemporary intellectuals, deduced that God had ordained social life to proceed within the structure of a 'family' or domestic unit. He proceeded, as they did not, to argue that the 'family' should be supported by an inalienable property, ruled by a paterfamilias with power of life and death, and dedicated through the generations to inculcating 'religion' in children and other subordinate members. Above families and father-governors would stand the *res publica* itself, a sovereign majesty absolute, perpetual and inviolable, issuing irresistible commands, in short—though Bodin did not say so—sacred. These attributes defined the public domain; without them there was no order, no security for the exercise of private domestic government or the cultivation of religion, only force and violence. As in the case of Thomas Hobbes, this theoretical structure certainly reflected an immediate context in which the rites of violence were being vigorously celebrated. But these do not exhaust its significance. What really matters about it is that it brought clarity to a transvaluation of values which had been in the making for quite a long time.

Forty years later, Bodin's view of the State, so modified as to bring a sacred political authority more obviously within the borders of Christian doctrine, had become the established political theory of the French monarchy. So it remained until the eighteenth century. Yet in the mean time the ultimate violation of his sanctuary of power, the act of tyrannicide, had not only been defended more vigorously than ever before; it had actually occurred in France in 1589 and in 1610, and very nearly occurred in England in 1605. The assassination of the Protestant William of Orange in 1584, and the execution of the Catholic Mary Queen of Scots in 1587, though neither could be classed as tyrannicide, showed that the transmigration of the sacred still had a long way to go. It was a good deal held up, and may in the end be said to have been frustrated, by some rather surprising developments in Spain. While Philip II bestrode the world, erected an American empire, and fought to defeat the resistance of his subjects in the Netherlands, those who wrote about political theory in his dominions were busy expounding the theme that no vestige of the sacred could be admitted amongst the attributes of monarchy. In the last year of the century one of them, Juan de Mariana, achieved European renown with an unruffled defence of tyrannicide. What they were implicitly conducting, like their predecessors in the days of Henry VIII and Catherine of Aragon, was a defence of the traditionally sacred: sapping the pretensions of English monarchs, casting doubt on the orthodoxy or sanity of the French, refuting what they supposed to be Lutheran positions. For Mariana the bishops, for his fellow-Jesuit Francisco de Suárez the pope, were at least for polemical purposes impregnable guardians of the sanctuary; Suárez furthermore, in one of the more interesting moves in the game, sought to expound a scheme of international sanctities which, like the circumnavigation of the Cape, would embarrass the enemy in its rear. How far these intellectual constructions corresponded to the state of affairs inside the dominions of Philip II or Philip III is a nice question. Most contemporary popes, and some Spanish bishops, would have been extremely sceptical; and it would be hard to deny that the Catholic kings had acquired since the days of Queen Isabella some odour of sanctity in the nostrils of their subjects, a thing which could not have been said of many of her ancestors. But a bird's eye view of Spanish civilisation would suggest that the Renaissance theorists had been fairly successful in their defensive strategy; their offensive campaign against the canonisation of the State stored up a good deal of ammunition for Locke.

For the moment its main effect in England, if one excludes the Gunpowder Plot itself, was to bring Suárez into public controversy with King James I. The progress of English or British ideas about the State, inevitably much affected by the Reformation, had become by 1600 even more dependent on developments in France. Throughout this period there was a close relation between theory and practice on the two sides of the Channel: during the 1590s, at the climax of controversy about the sacredness of monarchy in France, the principal affirmer was a Catholic Scot, William Barclay, and the principal doubter probably a Catholic Englishman, William Reynolds. (*De justa reipublicae Christianae in reges impios et haereticos authoritate*, 1590: if the author was not actually an Englishman, he had naturalised himself by borrowing the pseudonym Gullielmus Rossaeus from Thomas More.) Bodin himself had in 1581 played a small part in the English version of the drama, when he had declined to intervene in the case against the Jesuit missionary Edmund Campion. Campion was executed that December as party to a conspiracy to assassinate Queen Elizabeth allegedly hatched at the English College at Reims. This and later examples of the execution of justice in England, attended as they were by a ritual cuisine requiring dissection of the victim, boiling of entrails and placing of heads in public situations, might well be considered sacrificial rites in the temple of monarchy, a deity fancying the boiled where older gods preferred the roast.

They occurred in a context of the traditional English law of treason. Yet their occurrence fairly exactly spanned the period during which the instinctual grounds of political and religious conflict in England were undergoing the kind of subterranean shift I wish to describe. Seen in European perspective, the wars of the sacred in England were an offshoot of the state of affairs in France. At the beginning of their campaign, the defenders of English Catholicism stood on the ground, which they inherited from More, that royal supremacy over the Church was an indefensible violation of a system of exterior sanctities, a pollution of the sanctuary spreading contagion through the commonwealth. Among the consequences of this position was a judgement that all who entered such holy places of the Church of England as the ravages of the Turk had left standing, and participated however passively in the rites now being celebrated in them, became themselves unclean. To this frame of mind Pope Pius V's bull of 1570 against Queen Elizabeth was certainly congenial, and it finally exploded in a philippic against the queen by the Catholic leader William Allen, the *Admonition to the People of England and Ireland* issued from Rome in 1588 as the manifesto of a Spanish force of invasion. Yet by this time the ground had in fact changed: Allen's companion and successor Robert Parsons, who has had much the worse press of the two, was actually trying to do something more complicated. As a Jesuit, he found himself defending a spiritualised view of the Church which set less store by exterior sacrality and placed action before togetherness. At the same time he was driven to maintain, or to appear to maintain, a secular theory of the commonwealth in response to the rising tide of sanctified royalism. In this defensive posture and on this minimal axiom, that political arrangements were not 'matters of godhead and immortality', the most articulate exponent of Elizabethan Catholicism entered the seventeenth century. He and his colleagues were by now, quite apart from the prestige of Elizabeth and the successes of her government, faced with an interior erosion of their position which came from a tendency of many Catholics to flirt with the idea of sacred monarchy, and from the wholesale collapse which had overtaken all forms of monarchomachy in France. Several sources of monarcholatry converged on the English throne with the arrival of James VI from Scotland in 1603, and the unsuccessful attempt by Catholics in 1605 to blow to bits the arcana of British sovereignty provided James with an extremely favourable terrain for a confrontation about the sacredness of monarchy. His consequent debate about his oath of allegiance with Cardinal Bellarmine, Suárez and others, like similar arguments between the papacy and Venice, ensured the passage of the new model of the sacred from its birthplace in France to the Christian world at large.

An Act of Parliament passed in 1606 entitled the secular authorities in England to require Catholics to swear that they abhorred, as 'impious, heretical and damnable', the proposition that kings excommunicated by the pope might legitimately be deposed or assassinated. The adjectives were a bit haphazardly chosen, but evidently intended to bind Catholics to an idea of sacred monarchy assumed (optimistically, as it turned out) to be held by other Englishmen. In the ensuing argument no Catholic author, English or Continental, defended tyrannicide; over the pope's deposing power they divided between those who repudiated it absolutely and those who maintained it in theory but repudiated it in practice. Lay Catholics to whom the oath was presented usually proved willing to swear it. Despite many practical successes, on the theoretical front Catholicism was in retreat; the upshot of a spectacular controversy was roughly to vindicate Luther's opinion that there were two sorts of divinely ordained authority in the world, one of which was entitled to make rules about human society and the other was not. Bellarmine maintained that the Church was an externally structured *societas* or commonwealth invested by divine commission with all power requisite to achieve its end, the salvation of the souls of its members. As in his dealings with Galileo in 1616, Bellarmine was genuinely trying to limit the scope of godly interference in exterior matters: like Parsons, he had a sense of Christian *communitas* a good deal more restrictive, as well as more interior, than More's. But for monarchists his concessions were quite inadequate. They left intact a state within the State, authorised to pry at will into the actions of kings; and they ignored the fact that, in the state of plurality which Western Christendom had reached in 1600, a ruler was likely to be faced with a dozen conflicting godly admonitions, submission to any one of which would turn his kingdom into a battlefield. In the long run, civil society was the answer to the problem; for the moment, something more august was needed. Where Henry VIII and, probably, the Venetians looked back to an ultra-traditional source of sacred monarchy in the Christian Empire, the supporters of James I were able and indeed obliged to learn a lesson from the French, and reinvent the sacred from the civil.

The theory of divine right, said Figgis in *The Divine Right of Kings*, was the form in which the discovery of sovereignty was expressed in England. The position of English royalists in the early seventeenth century was that the facts about human society were much as St Augustine had supposed them: self-interest, partiality, hatred of enemies, an urge towards sociability turned catastrophic by the corruption of human nature. Unlike the medieval Church, and unlike their contemporary George Herbert, they did not see the institutions of Christianity as a saving machinery of social integration. They transmitted the prevailing view that the peace of Christ was not of this world, and that in a divided Christendom feelings about Christianity actually exacerbated private humour, partiality and conflict. God's ordinance for civil peace and the preservation of the human species from itself must therefore lie in universal submission to Government, and to sovereignty sacred and inviolable. Consecrated by the death of Charles I in 1649, in the midst of a shambles which might reasonably be felt experimental proof of the theory, this became the doctrine of the restored Church of England. Meanwhile two things had happened. The hypothesis that God had specified, in the institution of fatherhood, an obligatory form in which sacred sovereignty had been embodied and ought to be transmitted had been erected into a dogma in Sir Robert Filmer's *Patriarcha*; and the art of reinventing the sacred from the civil had achieved its masterpiece in Thomas Hobbes's mortal god, Leviathan.

(ii) Music

In finding a place for music among the transpositions of Christianity, we have two facts to start with. The first is that the modern Western musical tradition originated in the fifteenth century. The second is that the scene of this revolution in music was the composition of settings of the mass. As the creation of something new in European culture out of the tradition of sacramental Christianity, the event bears some resemblance to the sacralisation of the State. It is also, like the history of attitudes to the State, refreshingly difficult to classify according to conventional divisions of the period. The word 'renaissance' has been applied to it, but does not seem to shed much light. It occurred in the land of Huizinga, not in that of Burckhardt; classical humanists viewed it with distaste, and the majority of reformers did their best to strangle it. Most of those who contributed to it were extremely orthodox Catholics, and most of the remainder conservative Lutherans. It survived in the face of obstacles placed in its way by a cultural ethos dedicated to the cultivation of the word, proved fertile in secondary inventions, and finally erected after 1700 a whole new set of intellectual and social forms. These signs of vigour indicate the working of subterranean pressures of unusual force. Scepticism about whether a convincing account of them can ever be given is certainly in order: I can only say that I was tempted by the subject, and find it plausible to seek its context in the social history of Christianity.

There seem to be two genuine problems, one about function and one about form. There is also a spurious problem concerning the relations of music and text, which has received a good deal of attention but is probably a red herring drawn across the track by tone-deaf humanists. The functional problem is not just that music served the rites of Catholic Christendom and the texts associated with them, for plainsong did this and continued to do it. It concerns polyphony, and the place of polyphonic singing in a social conception of mass and the sacraments. Around 1400, by all accounts, polyphonic composition was expected to provide a suitably grand accompaniment for the ritual of festive occasions: either to recurring feasts which aroused particular devotion, or to occasions of particularly solemn celebration. One example is the motet *Supremum est mortalibus bonum* written in 1433 by the master of the French king's chapel, Guillaume Dufay, for the public reconciliation in Florence of Pope Eugenius IV and the future emperor Sigismund, after Sigismund had washed his hands of the anti-papal Council of Basel. It is in three voices, and at the end of what has been described as a 'rather bumpy' piece they join, in the sort of euphonious harmony which Dufay had borrowed from the English, to celebrate on a sequence of long-held notes the conjoined names of pope and king. The *supremum bonum* of the text is, inevitably, peace: in 1433 there was something to be said for the idea that the end of the conciliar movement might bring Christendom a bit of peace. Dufay responded in a similar vein to invitations to celebrate the marriage alliances of princes; he also made an effort to parallel the spatial harmonies embodied by Brunelleschi in the Duomo of Florence with a piece of peculiarly recondite integrative symbolism performed on the occasion of its consecration. Since the context of such particular celebrations was invariably a mass, it was natural that the setting of the mass itself should tend to conform to the style and spirit of the motet. It was the more natural since the forces required to perform the motet, which were both vocal and instrumental and often included a choirmaster with ambitions as a composer, had come by this date to constitute a part of the fixed establishment of major churches.

In the mass, polyphonic composition spread first from the occasional motet to what was called the proper, the variable texts related to particular feasts and votive purposes, and thence to the ordinary, or invariable texts. Yet it was from among the texts of the ordinary that polyphonists chose what became their favourite material and the site of the revolution in music. From 1450 or so the polyphonic composition of proper texts made little headway, even of those texts which were in very frequent use, like the mass for the dead. Meanwhile the setting of the ordinary became a matter of obsessive attention. This cannot be entirely put down to the need of a professional choir to have in its repertoire something it could sing repeatedly, for there can have been no shortage of opportunities to sing the mass for the dead. The principal reason must be that opportunities for integrated composition were found at hand in the corpus of texts of the ordinary which were not available in the proper. The opportunities would not have been there had not the mass been conceived as a social miracle.

The canon of five texts which after 1450 became the established foundation of the polyphonic mass was a selection made partly on musical and partly on ideological grounds. Composers were originally attracted by the larger items of the plainsong mass, the *Gloria* and *Credo*; but as they began to see them as part of a single whole the length of their texts, and especially of the *Credo* with its gritty dogmatic affirmations, came to be looked on as a nuisance. They shortened them by giving different sections to different voices to sing simultaneously, or by quietly omitting the drier parts. Since the first phrase of each continued to be sung by the priest in plainsong, these now became known as the *Et in terra* and the *Patrem*. Other, shorter and more singable texts received a corresponding expansion. The *Sanctus* became divided in two since it was now impossible to get it all in before the consecration, and a separate *Sanctus* and *Benedictus*, each with its concluding *Hosanna*, provided a frame for the elevation of the Host and an opportunity for something more devotionally expressive than the larger pieces. In plainsong masses the end was, naturally enough, the *Ite missa est*, and Guillaume de Machaut had used this in his first sketch of a polyphonic mass in the mid-fourteenth century. This was satisfying liturgically, but not artistically, and the place was taken by the *Agnus Dei,* a relative newcomer to the ordinary which had the advantage of a triple repetition, and above all of reconciling musical expression with theological and social meaning in its concluding *Dona nobis pacem*. This gave composers plenty to work on, and they used their expertise to turn it into an impressive finale. The *Agnus* also had the structural virtue of referring back to the beginning of the mass: the *Dona nobis* recapitulated the *Et in terra pax* at the opening of the *Gloria*. Earlier complete masses, particularly by English composers, began with *Et in terra*, so providing a thematic unity expressive of underlying theory. But on both musical and liturgical grounds it seems to have been felt that the *Gloria* was not quite the place to start; the *Kyrie*, with its triple invocation, was structurally very like the *Agnus*, and its penitential tone strengthened the darker element in an ensemble which would otherwise have been rather bland. Once the *Kyrie* had entered the composers' canon, its formal similarities with the *Agnus* invited them to integrate their compositions by carrying material from one to the other, though there were always, from Dufay to Bach, some who felt that the truer kinship was between the *Agnus* and the *Gloria*.

When the canon of texts was settled, and the compositional techniques developed for erecting upon it an audible symbol of plurality in unity, a new way of performing the integrative functions of the mass had been discovered. A mass by Dufay, or by his great Burgundian successor Josquin des Prés, was not *the* mass, but a parallel creation. It was an individual example of an artistic genre, which had an author and usually some other means of identification, and did not represent what was sung at any particular mass. Its most famous practitioners, like Josquin, were unwilling to compose for particular occasions and lax about meeting deadlines, and appreciated for the fact. By the end of the fifteenth century, volumes of Josquin's masses were appearing from the press in Venice. Had not the Reformation, and more especially the Counter-Reformation, intervened, it seems likely that by the end of the sixteenth century masses would have been written and performed outside a liturgical context, as they have come to be since.

This is not to say that the polyphonic mass was by 1500 falling outside the history of Christianity: though often composed upon secular melodies, it remained within the orbit of the sacred. Hence the vigour with which it was attacked and defended. Lollards had complained about polyphony. The Hussites repudiated it, seeing in its early developments, with some reason, a cacophony of self-absorbed voices giving audible witness to the disintegrated state of Christendom. They cultivated the monophonic hymn as they cultivated communion in both kinds. By 1500 humanists, obsessed by verbal culture, were saying much the same. Erasmus could find no warrant for polyphony in the scriptures, and thought that Christian music should be confined to psalm-singing, and not too much of that. His view was to dominate the attitude of most reformers in the sixteenth century, and to be influential on Catholics like More. It was left to Luther to expound the revolution which had led to Josquin as a creation of Christian feeling in its own right. Music, he held, was a divine gift only less precious than the Word itself. It was the master of the affections, the reconciler of strife and conflict. Polyphony, as practised by Josquin whom he idolised, was a supreme example of the integration of the many into the one, weaving its many voices and by implication the multitude of Christians into a fabric like a dance, a foretaste of the consort of the angels.

It was possible for Luther to take this view because in one central respect the theology of the 'mass' departed from the theology of the mass in the same way that his own did. The mass of Josquin and his contemporaries was all sacrament and no sacrifice. The canon was silent, and could not be set to music; the offertory, which as Luther said 'reeked of sacrifice', could be set in the form of a motet, but did not become part of an integrated mass-composition except in one instance. The exception, the requiem, was not in the repertoire of Renaissance composers; its invention was a post-Tridentine event inspired by Counter-Reformation insistence on the mass as a sacrifice. Hence, in the form which it had attained at the Reformation, the 'mass' could be regarded by Lutherans like Bach as a pure embodiment of the sacred. Here was surely a crucial translation. It was in the churches of Lutheran Germany that the institution of the 'spiritual concert', offering a diet of music for consumption by a body which was no longer exactly a congregation, but something more than an audience—in short, that the modern 'concert' was born, a quasi-sacred institution of modern times which by the mid-eighteenth century had spread through most of northern Europe, reformed or Catholic.

To proceed directly to that point is to cut a long story short and to omit most of what a history of music in the sixteenth and seventeenth centuries would include. But in what is not a history of music but an essay about Christianity it may seem the essential. On the Catholic side a comparable result was arrived at, but by a different route. Having lost Luther, the Catholic world was almost as vulnerable as reformed communities other than Luther's to the campaign of humanist criticism against polyphony. It obliterated the words, it made too much noise, it admitted vulgar passions into the arcana of religion. It was incompatible with prayer, a barbarous innovation which had no place in the synthesis of Christian and classical culture. Against this onslaught, musical theorists defended with dignity the independence and moral values of their art; they explained patiently that if you wanted harmony you must have diversity among its constituents, that a pure consonance could only make its point when dissonance preceded it. But they were supported neither by the progressive forces in the Church, Erasmians in style if not in substance, nor by the conservatives, who took it for granted that anything Luther approved of must be wrong. The romantic story goes that the Council of Trent proposed to abolish polyphony and was held back only by the evident divine inspiration of Palestrina's *Missa Papae Marcelli*. The first part of the story seems true, and as in other cases the Council eventually produced a compromise, which required a radical dissociation between the sacred and the secular in music. Its conception of the sacred in music was purely textual: sacred music was music to sacred texts. It must be subordinate to the texts, and to liturgical function in general, and must not include unseemly sounds, jumpy intervals or profane tunes. In the case of the mass the decision, in the short run, may claim credit for inspiring the ascetic master-pieces composed by Palestrina for the papal chapel; in the not very long run, that is by about 1600, it killed the genre by depriving it of nutrition and contrast. William Byrd, hidden away in the country houses of Jacobean England, was a late though passionate exception.

Forcibly dislodged from the mass, the imagination of Italian composers (of whom, after a dearth in the first creative period, there now appeared a glut), went into the invention of new forms within the now separated genres. They invented the sacred oratorio, the cantata and a new form of 'mass' which it inspired; they invented the secular madrigal, and opera. Opera, in a back-handed sort of way, fulfilled the humanist ambition to revive the music-drama of the ancients. As exemplified by Monteverdi's *Coronation of Poppaea* (1640), the parting of the secular and the sacred was good for invention but not so good for the soul, and maybe only the English will claim the oratorio as a respectable embodiment of the sacred. In general, the hobbling of sacred genres ensured a flight of musical talent towards secular ones. In the forms of secular music, as the vocal mode gave way before the instrumental, the exploration of the keys began to equip composers to evoke tension and resolution, on a scale Dufay and Josquin might have envied, in hearers whose need was no less urgent, though more private, than that of fifteenth-century Christendom.

(iii) Words

In a civilisation of the word, words are worth attention. At any time their meanings may shift, and shift in a meaningful way. At such a time their shifts may be symptoms of a general alteration in the processes of the mind, and evidence of historic change at a level otherwise remote from observation. It has been argued that one general alteration took place at the close of these three centuries; of those words whose meaning undoubtedly changed, several represented ideas and institutions at the heart of Christianity. The alteration which has been alleged by Michel Foucault was a change from what, as a Frenchman, he calls the 'Renaissance' to the 'classical' frame of mind, or roughly from the sixteenth to the seventeenth century. For our purposes it may seem effective on a larger scale of time. He defines it as a change from a mental procedure operating by resemblances, to one manipulating a system of identities and measurable differences. In the earlier universe things participated with each other, with the language which described them, and the persons who spoke of them; in the later universe they were classified into separate boxes, laid out as on a table by a language of conventional signs. Language segregated them, was itself segregated from the universe as a whole, and segregated individual minds from it and from each other. A universe ultimately harmonious, and inexhaustible since there was no limit to the affinities or antipathies which could be envisaged, was translated into a universe of finite, if often infinitesimal, difference.

The subject here has been the social not the physical universe, but to see the relevance of Foucault's imaginative invention we need go no further than some lines of an English traditionalist, a contemporary of Descartes and Galileo:

> Man is all symmetrie,
> Full of proportions, one limbe to another,
> And all to all the world besides.
> Each part may call the farthest brother,
> For hand with foot hath private amitie,
> And both with winds and tides.
>
> (George Herbert, 'Man')

To look for reasons which would make Herbert's version of the Christian universe hard for many to understand by the close of his century, we can consider the history during our period of some words which were for him venerable.

'Communion' in 1400 meant sharing, participation, community; in particular, within the Church; in particular, through the reception of the Eucharist; the act of receiving the Eucharist. By 1700 the first two meanings were still there, but were being superseded by 'distinct body of persons united by a common religious faith and rites'. The third and fourth were becoming 'sacramental union of the soul with Christ', while awaiting the transition to 'mystical contemplative union with nature'. 'Charity' in 1400 meant the state of Christian love or simple affection which one was in or out of regarding one's fellows; an occasion or body of people seeking to embody that state; the love of God, in both directions. In 1700 it meant an optimistic judgement about the good intentions of others; an act of benevolence towards the poor or needy; an institution erected as a result of such an act. In the second case the plural was possible from about 1600, in the third from about 1700. 'Conversation' in 1400 meant the state of living or behaving in an environment of other persons (in heaven, or with women) or of intimacy with things. To Samuel Johnson it meant 'the conveyance of thoughts reciprocally in talk'; it had been so used in the abstract from the late sixteenth century and in the concrete from the late seventeenth. One residual survival of the original meaning persisted in the law of adultery ('criminal conversation'). The word 'friend', perhaps Herbert's favourite, whose closeness to 'kinsman', objective and formal character, and status as one of a pair of opposites are essential memoranda in the description of traditional Christianity, was by 1700 approaching Johnson's 'one joined to another in mutual benevolence and intimacy'. To judge by the language of English politics in the eighteenth century ('the King's Friends') it had some way to go before reaching the goal. 'Amity' had become a relationship of states.

Of words which denoted the means of achieving such unifying states, and pointed to those passions which stood in their way, a displacement of the word 'penance' had been a message of Erasmus's New Testament. The English (and French) 'pay', which in 1400 had meant 'to make peace with, by providing some objective compensation or satisfaction, which might be monetary, for a claim' ('paid on both sides') and was a well-used term in the description of man's relation with his Creator, by 1700 meant 'to hand over money in return for goods or services', without any relation being created. It could not conceivably be used to refer to the relation of man and God. The word 'satisfaction' had shifted from the same point, but in a different direction, from meaning atonement to meaning (except for the duelling classes) contentment and gratification. By the mid-seventeenth century, 'satisfactory', which in its full sense had been a battlefield of the Reformation, had come to mean no more than its present 'reasonably adequate'. Unlike these, 'restitution' retained its original sense, but through the restriction of its bearing to questions of blood was declining in the direction of simple 'restoration'. The usage, which was also humanist, had been consecrated by the Authorised Version and by its application to the return of King Charles II.

We are surely bound to try to envisage such individual migrations as instances of a larger process: as, for example, symptoms of Foucault's archaeological shift in the ways of the mind, or of what has been called the process of civilisation. We could certainly do worse than envisage them as signs of transition from an ethics of solidarity to one of civility. If we believe that a change in Christianity must be an effect of some other change thought to be closer to the bone of human experience, we can point to the objectifying and delimiting process as having eventuated, within this period, in modern conceptions of property and the State; or, if we prefer, in a Holy Family which excluded such non-resident kin as John the Baptist. One objection to taking such changes to be nearer the bone than those already cited would be that, except in the case of the State, they do not seem to evoke any convincing motor event in the world of things: few, I guess, will be prepared to swallow the proposal that the emergence of 'market society' was such an event. Another objection is that, except again (probably) in the case of 'State', the transformation of the language of Christianity does not seem posterior, but if anything prior, to the transformation of language about other things.

As a partial instance of this priority, I offer the history of two words whose segregation and exterior relations are received ideas in modern culture. Shortly after 1400 the word 'religion', which had for centuries usually meant a 'religious' rule or order and those who followed or belonged to it, was revived by humanists to mean what it had meant in classical Latin, a worshipful attitude to God or a respect for holy things. 'Christian religion', as for Calvin, meant the primary posture of the Christian community, or of the individuals who composed it, towards God. There was argument about whether this posture did or did not entail an obligatory set of ritual observances and also, among cynics, about whether it was a profitable posture to be in at all. But nobody disputed that religion was an attribute of individuals or communities, or thought it something which existed apart from those who felt it or acted in accordance with it.

By 1700 the Christian world was full of religions, objective social and moral entities characterised by system, principles and hard edges, which could be envisaged by Voltaire as cutting one another's throats. Above their multiplicity planed a shadowy abstraction, *the* Christian Religion, and somewhere above that, in an upper region of the classifying system, religion with a capital 'R', planted in its new domain by people who did not usually feel or believe in it. The transition between the first universe of meaning and the second, though under way by 1600, took most of the seventeenth century to achieve: the *De veritate religionis Christianae* of the Dutch Arminian Hugo Grotius (1622) and in England William Chillingworth's *The Religion of Protestants* (1637) seem milestones along the road. Locke's usage exemplified it perfectly, Hobbes's did not. It looks a classic example of Foucault's linguistic shift, though it was in the first place a consequence of the multiplication of versions of the Christian faith.

In the fifteenth century 'society' meant a state of companionship, fellowship or mutually recognised relation with one or more of one's fellow men. Like 'religion' in the humanist sense, it was a term of art not a word of everyday life, and it was scarcely distinguished from friendship or charity except by being normally used in a different area of discourse. It could be used objectively, but not with much confidence and only in Latin. By 1700 or shortly after, it had already come to mean mainly an objective collectivity, exterior to its members and delimited from other such collectivities. Above them, as above the numerous examples of religion, planed the larger abstraction Society, an entity from which most actual human contact had been evacuated. The transition in this case may be dated between 1650 and 1700, and it too was an effect of the multiplication of Christian communities and a successor effect of the transition in 'religion', whose history it reproduced. One cannot therefore exactly call Religion and Society twins; but in other respects they are like the sexes according to Aristophanes, effects of the fission of a primitive whole, yearning towards one another across a great divide. The whole, for better or worse, was 'Christianity', a word which until the seventeenth century meant a body of people, and has since then, as most European languages testify, meant an 'ism' or body of beliefs.

Notes

1. E. Mâle, *L'Art religieux en France* (see Suggestions for Further Reading, Chap. 1), p. 146, n. 2.
2. *Dives and Pauper*, vol. i, part 1 (Early English Text Society, no. 275, London, 1976), pp. 31, 221.
3. F. R. H. Du Boulay, *An Age of Ambition* (London, 1970), p. 91.
4. K. L. Wood-Legh, *Perpetual Chantries in Britain* (Cambridge, 1965), p. 290.
5. P. Chaunu, 'Mourir à Paris (XVIe-XVIIe siècles)' *Annales E.S.C.*, xxxi (1976), p. 45.
6. J. Bossy, *The English Catholic Community, 1570–1850* (London, 1975), p. 271.
7. J. Hale, *Renaissance Europe, 1480–1520* (London, 1971), p. 121.
8. Quotations from P. Adam, *La Vie paroissiale en France au XIVe siècle* (Paris, 1964), p. 72; H. F. Westlake, *The Parish Gilds of Mediaeval England* (London, 1919), p. 68; G. M. Monti, *Le confraternite medio-evali dell'alta e media Italia* (2 vols., Venice, 1927), i, pp. 290–1.
9. A. Pastore, *Nella Valtellina nel tardo cinquecento: fede, cultura, società* (Milan, 1975), p. 58.
10. M. Bowker, *The Secular Clergy in the Diocese of Lincoln, 1495–1520* (Cambridge, 1968), pp. 120–1.
11. Thomas Walsingham, *Gesta abbatum monasterii sancti Albani* (3 vols., Rolls Series, 1867–9), iii, p. 309: a reference for which I am indebted to Dr R. J. Faith.
12. Bossy, *English Catholic Community* (n. 6 above), p. 262.
13. Suggestion made by Bernard Vogler in the course of a colloquium of the German Historical Institute London held at Wolfenbüttel, December 1981.
14. H. Thomas, *An Unfinished History of the World* (London, 1981 edn.), p. 292.
15. G. Bouchard, *Le Village immobile: Sennely-en-Sologne au XVIIIe siècle* (Paris, 1972), pp. 291–2.
16. Marvin B. Becker, 'Aspects of Lay Piety in Early Renaissance Florence', in Trinkaus and Oberman, *The Pursuit of Holiness* (see Suggestions for Further Reading: Part One), pp. 185–6.

17. *Les Entrées royales françaises de 1328 à 1515*, ed. B. Guenée and F. Lehoux (Centre Nationale de la Recherche Scientifique: Sources d'histoire médiévale, no. 5, Paris, 1968), pp. 241–65.

Suggestions for Further Reading

Part One: Traditional Christianity

Contact with historiographical tradition can be made through E. Delaruelle, E. - R. Labande and P. Ourliac, *L'Église au temps du Grand Schisme et de la crise conciliaire*, vol. xiv of A. Fliche, V. Martin, *et al.* (eds.) *Histoire de l'Église* (2 parts, Paris, 1962–4) or F. Rapp, *L'Église et la vie religieuse en Occident à la fin du Moyen Âge* (Nouvelle Clio; 2nd edn., Paris, 1980; bibliography). For individual countries: B. L. Manning, *The People's Faith in the Time of Wyclif* (Cambridge, 1919; repr. 1975); A. N. Galpern, 'The Legacy of Late Medieval Religion in Sixteenth-Century Champagne', in C. Trinkaus and H. Oberman (eds.), *The Pursuit of Holiness in Late Mediaeval and Renaissance Religion* (Leiden, 1974); B. Moeller, 'Piety in Germany on the Eve of the Reformation', in G. Strauss (ed.), *Pre-Reformation Germany* (London, 1972); J. Toussaert, *Le Sentiment religieux en Flandre à la fin du Moyen Âge* (Paris, 1965).

Outside history, I recommend A. van Gennep, *Manuel du folklore français contemporain*, esp. vol. i, parts 1–3 (Paris, 1943–7) and, from social anthropology, A. van Gennep, *The Rites of Passage* (London, 1960 edn.), J. Pitt-Rivers, 'The Kith and the Kin', in J. Goody (ed.), *The Character of Kinship* (Cambridge, 1973) and M. Douglas, *Purity and Danger* (London, 1970 edn.). E. Le Roy Ladurie, *Montaillou* (London, 1978 edn.) and, rather in spite of his intentions, C. Ginzburg, *The Cheese and the Worms* (London, 1980 edn.) convey similar insights into the traditional Christianity of this period. The handiest versions of its two classic written expressions are D. L. Sayers's and B. Reynolds's translation of *The Comedy of Dante Alighieri* (3 vols., London, 1949–62) and J. F. Goodridge's modern English version of William Langland, *Piers the Ploughman* (London, 1966 edn.).

Chapter 1

Anselm's *Cur Deus homo* is in J. - P. Migne (ed.), *Patrologia latina*, vol. clviii (Paris, 1858); theological commentary in G. Aulén, *Christus Victor* (London, 1970 edn.). The only fairly accessible text of Jacobus de Voragine's *The Golden Legend* is the French version of J. - B. M. Rose, *La*

Légende dorée (2 vols., Paris, 1967 edn.). The art historians are good value on the saints, particularly E. Mâle, *L'Art religieux en France à la fin du Moyen Âge* (5th edn., Paris, 1949) and M. Baxandall, *Painting and Experience in Fifteenth-Century Italy* (Oxford, 1972); so are I. Origo, *The World of San Bernardino* (London, 1963), on a contemporary saint; M. Warner, *Alone of All her Sex* (London, 1976), despite some nagging, on Our Lady; and J. - C. Schmitt, *Le Saint Lévrier* (Paris, 1979), on dogs.

Chapter 2

On **baptism:** J. D. C. Fisher, *Christian Initiation: Baptism in the Mediaeval West* (Alcuin Club, vol. xlvii, London, 1965), for texts and commentary, and J. Bossy, 'Blood and Baptism: Kinship, Community and Christianity in Western Europe, Fourteenth to Seventeenth Centuries', *Studies in Church History*, x (Oxford, 1973). On **marriage:** St Augustine, *The City of God*, book xv, chap. 16 (Everyman edn., 2 vols., London, 1945 edn.) is a fundamental text, J. - B. Molin and P. Mutembe, *Le Rituel de mariage en France du XIIe au XVIe siècle* (Paris, 1974) rich in detail. J. - L. Flandrin, *Les Amours paysannes* (Paris, 1975) is a humane and readable general account; C. Klapisch-Zuber, 'Zacharie, ou le père évincé', *Annales: Economies, Sociétés, Civilisations*, xxxiv (1979) and E. Le Roy Ladurie, *The Mind and Method of the Historian* (London, 1981), on the *aiguillette*, are brilliant on particulars. J. J. Scarisbrick, *Henry VIII* (London, 1968), chap. 7, is the classic analysis of a late medieval marriage case; H. Jedin, *Geschichte des Konzils von Trient*, vol. iv, part 2 (Freiburg-im-Breisgau, 1975), explains the decree of Trent.

On **death:** P. Ariès, *The Hour of our Death* (London, 1983 edn.) is worth comparing with N. Z. Davis, 'Some Tasks and Themes in the Study of Popular Religion', in *The Pursuit of Holiness* (above) and 'Ghosts, Kin and Progeny', in *Daedalus*, cvi, no. 2 (1977). On purgatory and masses for the dead, I liked J. Rosenthal, *The Purchase of Paradise* (London/Toronto, 1972) and M. and G. Vovelle, *Vision de la mort et de l'au-delà en Provence* (Cahiers des Annales, no. 29, Paris, 1970); on ghosts, K. Thomas, *Religion and the Decline of Magic* (London, 1971); on the dance of the dead, H. Rosenfeld, *Der mittelalterliche Totentanz* (2nd edn., Cologne/Graz, 1968), a complement to Mâle (above).

Chapter 3

M. W. Bloomfield, *The Seven Deadly Sins* (Ann Arbor, Mich., 1952) is a firm foundation; 'The Parson's Tale' is in *The Works of Geoffrey Chaucer*, ed. F. N. Robinson (London, 1957). J. Huizinga, *The Waning of the Middle Ages* (London, 1926 edn.), chap. 1; J. Burckhardt, *The Civilisation of the Renaissance in Italy* (London, 1951 edn.), part 6; Toussaert (above); and J. Rossiaud, 'Prostitution, jeunesse et société au XVe siècle', *Annales*

E.S.C., xxxi (1976) are the most interesting guides I have found to the conspectus of late medieval sin.

J. Caro Baroja, *El Carnaval: Análisis historico-cultural* (Madrid, 1965; French translation, *Le Carnaval*, Paris, 1979) is the only serious foundation for the study of the subject, except for van Gennep, *Manuel* (above); E. Le Roy Ladurie, *Carnival* (London, 1980 edn.) is the next best thing. **Penance** is treated carefully by T. F. Tentler, *Sin and Confession on the Eve of the Reformation* (Princeton, NJ, 1977) and speculatively by J. Bossy, 'The Social History of Confession in the Age of the Reformation', *Transactions of the Royal Historical Society*, 5th series, xxv (1975); both are indebted to H. C. Lea, *A History of Auricular Confession and Indulgences in the Latin Church* (3 vols., Philadelphia/London, 1896). On pilgrimage, A. Dupront, 'Pèlerinage et lieux sacrés', in *Mélanges en l'honneur de Fernand Braudel* (2 vols., Paris, 1973), is exciting on the theory, J. J. Jusserand, *English Wayfaring Life in the Middle Ages* (London, 1891 edn.) entertaining on the facts. When you have read R. W. Southern's account of indulgences in *Western Society and the Church in the Middle Ages* (London, 1970) and vol. iii of Lea's *History of Auricular Confession* you will probably be able to understand Luther's *Ninety-Five Theses* (in *Martin Luther: Selections from his Writings*, below).

Chapter 4

Dante's *La Vita Nuova* is in the original with an English translation in *La Vita Nuova and Canzoniere* (Temple Classics, London, 1906; repr. 1948). Delaruelle (above) is good on **fraternities**, and you might proceed via H. F. Westlake, *The Parish Gilds of Mediaeval England* (London, 1919), P. Duparc, 'Confréries du Saint-Esprit et communautés d'habitants au Moyen Âge', *Revue historique du droit français et étranger*, 4e série, xxxvi (1958) and M. - C. Gerbet, 'Les Confréries religieuses à Cacères de 1467 à 1523', *Mélanges de la Casa de Velasquez*, vii (Paris, 1971) to B. Pullan's classic *Rich and Poor in Renaissance Venice* (Oxford, 1971).

On **priests and parishes** you can avoid cliché with the help of P. Heath, *The English Parish Clergy on the Eve of the Reformation* (London/Toronto, 1969); L. Binz, *Vie religieuse et réforme ecclésiastique dans le diocèse de Genève, 1378–1450*, vol. i (Geneva, 1973); C. de la Roncière, 'Les Communautés chrétiennes et leurs curés', in Delumeau (ed.), *Histoire vécue du peuple chrétien*, vol. i (below); G. R. Elton, 'Tithe and Trouble', in *Star Chamber Stories* (London, 1958); and H. C. Lea, *A History of Sacerdotal Celibacy in the Latin Church* (3rd edn., 2 vols., London, 1907).

On the **mass**, J. A. Jungmann, *The Mass of the Roman Rite* (2 vols., New York, 1951–5) provides the liturgical history; J. Bossy, 'The Mass as a Social Institution, 1200–1700', *Past and Present*, no. 100 (1983), offers an interpretation; and N. J. Perella, *The Kiss, Sacred and Profane* (Berkeley,

Cal., 1969) should not be missed. On the Eucharist, P. Browe, *Die Verehrung der Eucharistie im Mittelalter* (Munich, 1933; repr. Darmstadt, 1967). On Corpus Christi and public ritual in general there are fine pieces by M. E. James, 'Ritual, Drama and Social Body in the late Mediaeval English Town', *Past and Present*, no. 98 (1983); B. Moeller, 'Imperial Cities and the Reformation', in his *Imperial Cities and the Reformation* (Philadelphia, 1972); C. Phythian-Adams, 'Ceremony and the Citizen: the Communal Year at Coventry, 1450–1550', in P. Clark and P. Slack (eds.), *Crisis and Order in English Towns, 1500–1700* (London, 1978). N. Z. Davis, 'The Rites of Violence', *Past and Present*, no. 59 (1973), is another classic.

On '**magic**': Thomas, *Religion and the Decline of Magic* (above); A. Franz, *Die kirchlichen Benediktionen im Mittelalter* (2 vols., Freiburg-im-Breisgau, 1909); W. A. Christian, *Local Religion in Sixteenth-Century Spain* (Princeton, NJ, 1981), a pathfinder on vows.

Chapter 5

J. N. Hillgarth, *The Spanish Kingdoms, 1250–1516* (2 vols., Oxford, 1976–8) is quite outstanding for relations with Moors and Jews; I. Abrahams, *Jewish Life in the Middle Ages* (2nd edn., London, 1932) gives the view from inside; B. Pullan, *The Jews of Europe and the Inquisition of Venice* (Oxford, 1983) adds this dimension to his discussion in *Rich and Poor*, which is also good on usury. B. Nelson, *The Idea of Usury* (2nd edn., Chicago/London, 1969) is a small jewel.

The literary sources on **witchcraft** are collected in H. C. Lea, *Materials towards a History of Witchcraft* (3 vols., New York/London, 1957). For the pre-Reformation history, W. A. Monter, *Witchcraft in France and Switzerland* (Ithaca, NY, 1976); N. Cohn, *Europe's Inner Demons* (London, 1975); and, above all, R. Kieckhefer, *European Witchtrials, 1300–1500* (London, 1976).

On **heretics**: G. Leff, *Heresy in the Later Middle Ages* (2 vols., Manchester/New York, 1967) is more intellectual, M. Lambert, *Mediaeval Heresy* (London, 1977) more factual; Lambert is particularly good on the Bohemians. N. Cohn, *The Pursuit of the Millennium* (London, 1970 edn.); J. A. F. Thomson, *The Later Lollards, 1414–1520* (London, 1965); and P. Brock, *The Political and Social Doctrines of the Unity of Czech Brethren* (The Hague, 1957) are all good value in different ways.

Part Two: Christianity Translated

Beginners might start with H. Grimm, *The Reformation Era* (New York, 1965 edn.). J. Delumeau, *Le Catholicisme entre Luther et Voltaire* (Nouvelle Clio, Paris, 1971; English translation, without the bibliography, *Catholic-*

ism between Luther and Voltaire, London, 1978) suggests a more long-term view, which can be explored from various angles in: P. Collinson, *The Religion of Protestants* (Oxford, 1982); H. O. Evennett, *The Spirit of the Counter-Reformation* (Cambridge, 1968); J. Delumeau (ed.), *Histoire vécue du peuple chrétien* (2 vols., Paris, 1979); and M. Roberts, 'The Swedish Church', in M. Roberts (ed.), *Sweden's Age of Greatness, 1632–1718* (London, 1973).

Chapter 6

i. For the Reformation doctrine of the Atonement, J. Rivière, art. 'Rédemption', in *Dictionnaire de théologie catholique*, xiii (Paris, 1937) and Aulén (above). My analogy of law can be judged with the help of B. Lenman and G. Parker, 'The State, the Community and the Criminal Law in Early Modern Europe', in V. A. C. Gattrell, *et al.* (eds.), *Crime and the Law: The Social History of Crime in Western Europe since 1500* (London, 1980).

R. H. Bainton, *Here I Stand* (New York, 1955 edn.) and *Martin Luther: Selections from his Writings*, ed. J. Dillenberger (Garden City, NY, 1961) will do for a start on Luther; F. Wendel, *Calvin* (London, 1965 edn.) and *The Institutes of the Christian Religion*, ed. J. T. McNeill (Library of Christian Classics, vols. xx–xxi, Philadelphia, 1967) on Calvin; P. Mack Crew, *Calvinist Preaching and Iconoclasm in the Netherlands, 1544–69* (Cambridge, 1978) on image-smashing; A. Blunt, *Artistic Theory in Italy, 1450–1600* (Oxford, 1940) and R. Wittkower, *Art and Architecture in Italy, 1600–1750* (3rd edn., London, 1973) on the arts in the Counter-Reformation.

ii. R. H. Bainton, *Erasmus of Christendom* (London, 1972 edn.) and *The Essential Erasmus*, ed. J. P. Dolan (New York, 1964) introduce the master of humanist Christianity; C. Trinkaus, *In Our Own Image and Likeness* (2 vols., London, 1970) relates its Italian origins; G. Potter, *Zwingli* (Cambridge, 1976) and R. Stupperich, *Melanchthon* (London, 1966 edn.) present two reformers of humanist inclinations.

On scripture and tradition, Thomas More, *Confutation of Tyndale*, in *The Complete Works of St Thomas More*, vol. viii (New Haven/London, 1973); G. H. Tavard, *The Seventeenth-Century Tradition* (Leiden, 1978). E. Eisenstein, *The Printing Press as an Agent of Change* (Cambridge, 1980 edn.) has a rather thumping account of the effects of typography on Christianity; W. Ong, *The Presence of the Word* (New Haven/London, 1967) is the most interesting of the more theoretical approaches. L. Febvre and H. - J. Martin, *The Coming of the Book* (London, 1976) and M. Aston, 'Lollardy and Literacy', *History*, lxii (1977) are in a class of their own. For the Apocalypse as seen by a master of the visual aid, E. Panofsky, *The Life and Art of Albrecht Dürer* (Princeton, NJ, 1971 edn.).

180   *Suggestions for Further Reading*

iii. On the German side, the radical texts are collected in *Spiritual and Anabaptist Writers*, ed. G. H. Williams and A. M. Mergal (Library of Christian Classics, vol. xxv, Philadelphia, 1957). G. H. Williams, *The Radical Reformation* (Philadelphia, 1962) is ponderous but essential. I found S. E. Ozment, *Mysticism and Dissent* (New Haven/London, 1973) very convincing on the ideas, C. P. Clasen, *The Anabaptists: A Social History, 1525–1618* (Ithaca/London, 1972) on the people.

On the English side, the writings of the Ranters are given in extensive extracts in Cohn, *The Pursuit of the Millennium* (above) and most of Winstanley's in G. Winstanley, *The Law of Freedom and Other Writings*, ed. C. Hill (London, 1973; Cambridge, 1983). G. F. Nuttall, *The Holy Spirit in Puritan Faith and Experience* (Oxford, 1946) puts in what C. Hill, *The World Turned Upside-Down* (London, 1972) and *The Religion of Gerrard Winstanley* (*Past and Present* Supplement, Oxford, 1978) leave out. B. Capp, *The Fifth Monarchy Men* (London, 1972) and K. Thomas, 'Women and the Civil War Sects', in T. Aston (ed.) *Crisis in Europe, 1560–1660* (London, 1965) are sane and lively.

Chapter 7

i. The texts on baptism are in J. D. C. Fisher, *Christian Initiation: The Reformation Period* (Alcuin Club, vol. li, London, 1970), Luther's 'Shorter Catechism' in *Documents of the Continental Reformation*, ed. B. J. Kidd (Oxford, 1914, repr. 1967). Various traditions of catechizing are dealt with by G. Strauss, *Luther's House of Learning* (Baltimore/London, 1975), or his 'Success and Failure in the German Reformation', *Past and Present*, no. 67 (1975) (unenthusiastic); by J. - C. Dhotel, *Les Origines du catéchisme moderne* (Paris, 1967), C. Hill, *Society and Puritanism in Pre-Revolutionary England* (London, 1964), and L. Pérouas, *Le Diocèse de la Rochelle de 1648 à 1724* (Paris, 1964). N. Elias, *The Civilizing Process* (Oxford, 1978) and P. Ariès, *Centuries of Childhood* (London, 1962 edn.) sketch the history of civility.

Connections between Christianity and demographic history are explored in articles by A. Burguière and J. - L. Flandrin, in R. Forster and P. Ranum (eds.), *Family and Society: Selections from Annales* (Baltimore/London, 1976). J.- L. Flandrin, *Families in Former Times* (Cambridge, 1979 edn.) is the nicest introduction to the early modern family; L. Stone, *The Family, Sex and Marriage in England, 1500–1800* (London, 1977) is important but overemphatic. J. T. Noonan, *Contraception* (Cambridge, Mass., 1966) is indispensable. The literature of advice to couples can be sampled in K. M. Davies, 'The Sacred Condition of Equality', *Social History*, no. 5 (1977).

ii. The ur-text of Reformation *disciplina* is M. Bucer, *De regno Christi*, ed. F. Wendel (2 vols., Paris/Gütersloh, 1954–5); B. Vogler and J. Estèbe, 'La

Genèse d'une société protestante', *Annales E.S.C.*, xxxi (1976) and T. C. Smout, *A History of the Scottish People, 1560–1830* (London, 1972 edn.) illustrate its effects on the ground. The rise of the sabbath can be followed in P. Collinson, 'The Beginnings of English Sabbatarianism', *Studies in Church History*, vol. i (Oxford, 1964) and Hill, *Society and Puritanism* (above). For Protestant fasting, see H. R. Trevor-Roper, 'The Fast Sermons of the Long Parliament', in his *Religion, the Reformation and Social Change* (below). J. Bossy, 'The Counter-Reformation and the People of Catholic Europe', *Past and Present*, no. 47 (1970) is an introduction to Catholic *disciplina*; Evennett, *Spirit of the Counter-Reformation* (above) and Bossy, 'The Social History of Confession' (above) explore the upper and lower reaches of Catholic *metanoia*. O. C. Watkins, *The Puritan Experience* (London, 1972) is moving and exact on its Protestant counterpart.

Early modern sin has proved more refractory to system than medieval: M. E. James, *English Politics and the Concept of Honour, 1485–1642 (Past and Present* Supplement, Oxford, 1978) (obedience); M. Foucault, *Histoire de la sexualité*, vol. i (Paris, 1975) (sex); and J. Delumeau, *Le Péché et la peur* (Paris, 1983) (fear) are three attempts to introduce it. I prefer the first.

S. Anglo (ed.), *The Damned Art* (London, 1977) discusses the contemporary texts on witchcraft, H. R. Trevor-Roper, 'The European Witch-Craze of the Sixteenth and Seventeenth Centuries', in his *Religion, the Reformation and Social Change* (London, 1967) and Thomas, *Religion and the Decline of Magic* (above) represent with distinction opposite ends of the interpretative range. H. C. E. Midelfort, *Witch-hunting in South-West Germany, 1562–1684* (Stanford, Cal., 1972) and C. Larner, *Enemies of God: The Witch-Hunt in Scotland* (London, 1981) strike me as the best regional investigations; explanation by culture- or class-conflict is offered, for example, by C. Ginzburg, *The Night Battles* (London, 1983).

iii. Y. Brilioth, *Eucharistic Faith and Practice* (London, 1930 edn.) is essential on the Eucharist, R. Gough, *The History of Myddle*, ed. D. Hey (London, 1981) on pews. The student of early modern charity ought to start with B. Tierney, *The Mediaeval Poor Law* (Berkeley/Los Angeles, 1959) and will have to slog through W. K. Jordan, *Philanthropy in England, 1480–1660* (London, 1959), and sample its regional offspring. After this he can be rewarded with Pullan, *Rich and Poor in Renaissance Venice* (above) and 'Catholics and the Poor in Early Modern Europe', *Transactions of the Royal Historical Society*, 5th series, xxvi (1976); J. Gutton, *La Société et les pauvres: l'exemple de la généralité de Lyon, 1534–1789* (Paris, 1969); E. Grendi, 'Pauperismo e Albergo dei Poveri nella Genova del seicento', *Rivista storica italiana*, lxxxvii (1975); and K. Wrightson and D. Levine, *Poverty and Piety in an English Village:*

Terling, 1525–1700 (London/New York, 1979). M. Foucault, *Madness and Civilisation* (London, 1971 edn.) will provide a lively conclusion. Searchers for the Protestant ethic should look at Baxter's *Christian Directory* (see text) before trying M. Weber, *The Protestant Ethic and the Spirit of Capitalism* (2nd edn. with intro. by A. Giddens, London, 1976), K. Samuelsson, *Religion and Economic Action* (Stockholm/London, 1961), and much more.

Chapter 8

The history of political holiness can be followed in Thomas More, *The History of King Richard III*, in *The Complete Works of St Thomas More*, vol. ii (New Haven/London, 1963); Luther, *On Secular Authority*, in *Selections from his Writings* (above); J. Bodin, *Six Books of the Commonwealth* (abridged translation by M. J. Tooley, Oxford, [1955]) and *The Political Works of James I*, ed. C. H. McIlwain (Cambridge, Mass., 1918), not to mention Sir Robert Filmer and Thomas Hobbes. Q. Skinner, *The Foundations of Modern Political Thought*, vol. ii, *The Reformation* (Cambridge, 1978) provides most of what is needed by way of commentary. J. Bossy, 'The Character of Elizabethan Catholicism', in T. Aston (ed.), *Crisis in Europe, 1560–1660* (above) is an introduction to the politics of the subject.

A. Robertson and D. Stevens (eds.), *The Pelican History of Music*, vol. ii, *Renaissance and Baroque* (London, 1963) is accessible to the unprofessional, and O. Strunk (ed.), *Source Readings in Music History* (London, 1952) a fine collection of contemporary texts. The article 'Messe' in *Die Musik in Geschichte und Gegenwart*, ed. F. Blume, vol. ix (Kassel, etc., 1961) is most informative. I do not know quite what to recommend about words, but report that I have consulted the *Oxford English Dictionary* under the guidance of M. Foucault, *The Order of Things* (London, 1970 edn). Some of the relevant words are discussed in my 'Some Elementary Forms of Durkheim', *Past and Present*, no. 95 (1982); others in the 'Conclusion' of Skinner, *Foundations* and in Flandrin, *Families* (both above).

Index